Econometric Methods for Labour Economics

Practical Econometrics

Series Editors
Jurgen Doornik and Bronwyn Hall

Practical econometrics is a series of books designed to provide accessible and practical introductions to various topics in econometrics. From econometric techniques to econometric modelling approaches, these short introductions are ideal for applied economists, graduate students, and researchers looking for a non-technical discussion on specific topics in econometrics.

Books published in this series

An Introduction to State Space Time Series Analysis
Jacques J. F. Commandeur and Siem Jan Koopman

Non-Parametric Econometrics
Ibrahim Ahamada and Emmanuel Flachaire

Econometric Methods for Labour Economics
Stephen Bazen

Econometric Methods for Labour Economics

Stephen Bazen

OXFORD
UNIVERSITY PRESS

OXFORD
UNIVERSITY PRESS

Great Clarendon Street, Oxford OX2 6DP

Oxford University Press is a department of the University of Oxford.
It furthers the University's objective of excellence in research, scholarship,
and education by publishing worldwide in

Oxford New York

Auckland Cape Town Dar es Salaam Hong Kong Karachi
Kuala Lumpur Madrid Melbourne Mexico City Nairobi
New Delhi Shanghai Taipei Toronto

With offices in

Argentina Austria Brazil Chile Czech Republic France Greece
Guatemala Hungary Italy Japan Poland Portugal Singapore
South Korea Switzerland Thailand Turkey Ukraine Vietnam

Published in the United States
by Oxford University Press Inc., New York

First published 2011

British Library Cataloguing in Publication Data
Data available

Library of Congress Cataloging in Publication Data
Library of Congress Control Number: 2011934701

Typeset by SPI Publisher Services, Pondicherry, India
Printed in Great Britain
on acid-free paper by
MPG Books Group, Bodmin and King's Lynn

ISBN 978–0–19–957679–1

5 7 9 10 8 6 4

Acknowledgements

I am very grateful to Xavier Joutard and three anonymous referees for their helpful comments and criticisms of earlier versions of the material presented here. I would also like to thank Bronwyn Hall for her suggestions. I bear full responsibility for any errors and any lack of clarity in the text. At Oxford University Press, I wish to thank Sarah Caro for her support in initiating this project. I am especially grateful to Aimee Wright for her work in bringing the final product into existence. On a personal level, I would like to thank Marie-Pierre, Laura, and Matthieu for their support and understanding during the period in which I wrote the different versions of this book.

Marseilles, December 2010

Contents

List of Figures

List of Tables

Data Sources

The examples in the text are based data made available to researchers by national statistical agencies and certain institutions. Three sources have been used:

British Household Panel Survey

For access it is necessary to register online and the files can be downloaded once authorization is given (www.data-archive.ac.uk).

Enquête Emploi

This is the French Labour Force Survey and can be accessed by downloading and signing a 'conditions of use' agreement. Data are then made available by file transfer (www.cmh.ens.fr).

Merged CPS Outgoing Rotation Group Compact Disc

I purchased this compact disc from the National Bureau for Economic Research (www.nber.org).

There are now a large number of data sets available for analysing labour market phenomena. The Luxemburg Income Study and its successors is a very useful source (www.lisproject.org). Most national statistical agencies now allow researchers to have free access to labour force surveys and certain surveys that contain more detailed data on earnings.

Introduction

A labour economist, whether in training or fully qualified, will either be undertaking or need to be able to read empirical research. As in other areas of economics, there are a number of econometric techniques and approaches that have come be regarded as 'standard' or part of the labour economist's toolkit. It is noteworthy that many modern econometric techniques have been specifically developed to deal with a situation encountered in applied labour economics. These methods are now covered to differing degrees and at various levels of complexity in a number of econometrics texts alongside the more general material on estimation and hypothesis testing.

One of the specificities of labour economics is the use of micro-data, by which we generally mean data on individuals, households, and firms, that is data corresponding to the notion of 'economic agent' in microeconomic analysis. There now exist a number of excellent econometrics texts that deal with methods for analysing such data—two recent examples are *Microeconometrics: Methods and Applications*, by C. Cameron and P. Trivedi and *Econometrics with Cross Section and Panel Data*, by J. Wooldridge. There are equally chapters in the series *Handbook of Labor Economics* that treat many aspects of undertaking of empirical research in labour economics, as well as excellent survey papers in the *Journal of Economic Literature* and the *Journal of Econometrics*. There is also the book by J. Angrist and J.S. Pischke, *Mostly Harmless Econometrics*, which in recent years has become an important reference for labour economists. These are all excellent references but they have a fairly high 'entry fee' in terms of substantial familiarity with a number of econometric techniques and statistical concepts.

The current book has the modest aim providing a *practical* guide to understanding and applying the standard econometric tools that are used in labour economics. Emphasis is placed on both the input and the output of empirical analysis, rather than the understanding of the origins and properties of estimators and tests, topics which are more than adequately covered in recent textbooks on microeconometrics. In my experience of teaching econometrics at all levels, including a graduate course on econometric applications in labour economics, there is a noticeable difference between students' capacity to understand the material presented in a lecture and their ability to apply it and produce a competent piece of empirical work using real world data. It is a little reminiscent of Edward Leamer's description of the teaching of econometric principles on the top floor of the faculty building and applying them in the computer laboratory in the basement, and how in moving between the two, the instructors underwent an academic Jekyll and Hyde-like transformation (Leamer, 1978). As he put it a little later: 'There are two things you are better off not watching in the making: sausages and econometric estimates' (Leamer, 1983, p. 37). Matters have evolved somewhat since that time. Data sets have become richer and more accessible; computer technology has removed most of the constraints that weigh on estimating nonlinear models with large samples; econometric techniques have become more sophisticated; numerous empirical studies on a given topic coexist; and replication and meta-analysis have become commonplace.

This book is aimed at providing practical guidance in moving from the econometric methods commonly used in empirical labour economics to their application. It can be used as a reference on postgraduate (and possibly undergraduate) courses, as an aid for those beginning to do empirical research, and as a refresher for researchers who wish to apply a tool they know of but have not yet used in their own research. It is not a guide to cutting-edge research, nor is it an applied econometrics textbook.

The basic idea developed in this book is that linear regression is an important starting point for empirical analysis in labour economics. By linear regression, I mean estimating by a least squares type estimator, the parameters (the β's) of a relation of the following form:

$$y_i = x_{1i}\beta_1 + \ldots. + x_{ki}\beta_k + u_i$$

where i refers to the observation unit (individual, firm, region etc), y_i is the variable to be modelled, $x_{1i}, x_{2i}, x_{3i} \ldots x_{Ki}$ are explanatory variables and u_i is the error term. Most of the more sophisticated methods commonly used in labour economics have their origin in a problem encountered when seeking to use a linear regression model with a particular type of data. Even when a nonlinear approach is appropriate, the function adopted is more often than not defined on a linear index, that is $(x_{1i}\beta_1 + \ldots. + x_{ki}\beta_k)$, so that many aspects of model specification and interpretation carry over. Emphasis is placed on how we can obtain reliable estimates of these parameters and how we can use them to make statements about labour market phenomena.

The applications presented are all based on real-world data, data which are freely available to researchers from the various national statistical agencies and data archives. I cannot make the data available myself due to conditions of access but I have provided a list on p. xi of this book of where individual researchers can obtain the data.

This book is written on the understanding that the reader already has some knowledge of basic econometrics. Where I have needed to derive a technical result that is useful for understanding why a model or estimator may be unreliable or take on a particular form, I have presented the details in an accessible form in appendices to the chapters. Since there are a large number of variants of particular models, in order to convey as much useful information as possible concerning the use of a model and the interpretation of the results it provides, I present what I regard to be the 'standard' version of the model. In practice, depending on the nature of the data being used, the standard model may need to be adapted. The variants are usually available as options in the procedures in commonly used software programs.

1

The Use of Linear Regression in Labour Economics

While econometric techniques have become increasingly sophisticated, regression analysis in one form or another continues to be a major tool in empirical studies. Linear regression is also important in the way it serves as a reference for other techniques—it is usually the failure of the conditions that justify the application of linear regression that give rise to alternative methods. Furthermore, many more complicated techniques often contain elements of linear regression or modifications of it. In this chapter and the following one, the use of linear regression and related methods in labour economics is covered.

A key application in labour economics where regression is used is the estimation of a Mincer-type earnings equation where the logarithm of earnings is regressed on a constant, a measure of schooling and a quadratic function of labour market experience (see Mincer, 1974, and Lemieux, 2006). Consider the following regression estimates for the United States which are examined more closely in a later section of this chapter:

$$\begin{aligned} \log w_i &= \underset{(0.01)}{0.947} + \underset{(0.0007)}{0.074}\, s_i + \underset{(0.0005)}{0.041}\, ex_i - \underset{(0.000013)}{0.00075}\, ex_i^2 + \text{residual} \\ R^2 &= 0.24 \qquad \hat{\sigma} = 0.39 \qquad n = 80201 \end{aligned}$$

where w_i is hourly earnings, s_i years of education, and ex_i years of labour market experience. The figures in parentheses are estimated standard errors and the ratio of the coefficient estimate to its corresponding standard error is the t statistic for the null hypothesis that the parameter in question is equal to zero.

This is a typical earnings equation in labour economics with typical results. The estimated equation yields the following information. First, all the coefficients are highly significantly different from zero since their absolute t statistics are more than fifty times the 5% critical value of 1.96. Second, the R^2 is particularly low—in both absolute terms and relative to values found in time series applications. It suggests that human capital differences explain only a quarter of log earnings differences between individuals. Third, the return to an additional year of education is estimated to be approximately 7.5%. Fourth, the return to a year's extra labour market experience is decreasing with experience since the function is concave. In the first year in the labour force, other things being equal, earnings rise by roughly 4.1% on average. For someone with 10 years of accumulated experience, the return to 1 more year is 2.6%, declining to 1.1% after 20 years experience, and becoming negative after 27 years. Fifth, the estimated constant suggests that (if such an individual exists) someone entering the labour market for the first time with no educational investment will on average have hourly earnings of $\$2.58 = \exp(0.948)$.

These different statements about the determinants of earnings are only valid if the earnings equation is not misspecified and if the conditions under which ordinary least squares estimation provides reliable results are met. In the first section of this chapter, a number of basic results concerning estimation and hypothesis testing in the linear model are reviewed. This is followed in the second section by a description of different sources of misspecification, how these can be diagnosed, and what can be done when misspecification is detected. In the third section the Mincer earnings equation is re-examined in terms of data requirements, interpretation of the parameters, and specification issues.

1.1 The Linear Regression Model—A Review of Some Basic Results

In order to have a basis for developing different approaches, a number of useful results on the linear regression model are presented in this section. Excellent modern treatments of the details in a specifically cross-section context can be found in Wooldridge (2002) and Cameron and Trivedi (2005).

The linear regression model is written as:

$$y_i = x_i'\beta + u_i$$

where i refers to the observation unit (individual, firm, region etc), y_i is the variable to be modelled or the dependent variable, $x_i' = (1 \quad x_{2i}, x_{3i} \ldots x_{Ki})$ is a line vector of explanatory variables or regressors (the prime indicates 'transpose') with an associated column vector of K unknown parameters β, and u_i is the error term.

1.1.1 *Interpretations of Linear Regression*

One of the main aims of econometric analysis is to obtain a 'good' estimate of each of the elements of the vector β from a sample of n observations, where values of each variable $\{y_i, x_i'\}$ are recorded for each observation (for example, each individual). A given parameter in this vector, say β_k, can be given a number of interpretations. In a cross-section context, the following would seem appropriate:

(i) If we treat the systematic component as the conditional expectation of y_i on x_i that is $E(y_i|x_i) = x_i'\beta$ and $E(u_i) = 0$, then β_k is simply the partial derivative of this conditional expectation with respect to x_k:

$$\beta_k = \frac{\partial E(y_i|x_i)}{\partial x_k}$$

β_k is thus the effect of a small increase in x_k on the average value of y other things being equal. This is often referred to as the *marginal effect* of x_k on y. The linearity of the conditional expectation means that each coefficient β_k, being a partial derivative, is simply the slope of a straight line relating the average value of y and x_k for given values of the other explanatory variables. Implicit in this interpretation is that a change in x_k involves a movement along (upwards or downwards) that straight line. While this has intuitive appeal for variables that change over time, it is less intuitive when the variation in x_k is a change in an individual's characteristics of profile. For example, interpreting the coefficient as a marginal effect amounts to saying that an individual who experiences a change in characteristic x_k will move to an earnings level corresponding to what others with that value of the characteristic generally earn. Furthermore, being expressed as a partial derivative, interpreting a coefficient in this way means that it is only relevant for continuous variables. For dummy variables, the coefficient can be interpreted as a marginal effect as the variation in the earnings of an individual with mean characteristics with and without the characteristic represented by dummy (for example, being a trade union member or not).

(ii) A second interpretation of the coefficients of a regression, and one that lends itself best to the analysis of the behaviour of economic agents, is by taking two agents who are in all respects identical (including $u_i = u_j$) except that for one the variable x_{ki} takes the value $\tilde{x}_{ki}$, and for the second $x_{kj} = \tilde{x}_{ki} + 1$. The difference between the two values of y is then:[1]

$$y_j - y_i = \beta_k$$

[1] The difference in the dependent variable between the two individuals is $y_i - y_j = \sum_{m \neq k} x_{mi}\beta_m + \tilde{x}_{ki}\beta_k + u_i - \sum_{m \neq k} x_{mj}\beta_m - (\tilde{x}_{ij} + 1)\beta_k - u_j$. If the individuals are identical in all other respects then $\sum_{m \neq k} x'_{mi}\beta_m = \sum_{m \neq k} x'_{mj}\beta_m$ and $u_i = u_j$, so that $y_i - y_j = \beta_k$.

This is the *counter-factual* interpretation of the coefficient β_k. If the value of x_k for individual j is one unit higher than that of the otherwise identical individual i, (s)he will have a value of y which is β_k higher than individual i. This interpretation seems natural for cross-section analysis and avoids the problem of interpreting parameters as derivatives when the explanatory variable is not continuous, as in the case of dummy variables and integer variables. The marginal effect defined earlier is for an individual with *average* characteristics. In the counter-factual approach, the coefficient is interpreted for two *identical* individuals but for the altered characteristic. The two interpretations coincide for two individuals with average characteristics (that is identical observed characteristics) since

$$E\left(y_j - y_i\right) = \beta_k + E\left(u_j - u_i\right) = \beta_k$$

due to the hypothesis that the error term has a zero mean.

1.1.2 *Estimation*

If we have a sample of n observations on $\left(y_i, x_i'\right)$, the OLS estimator of the vector β is expressed in matrix terms as

$$\hat{\beta} = \left(X'X\right)^{-1} X'y$$

where $y' = \left(y_1, y_2, y_3 \ldots y_n\right)$, $X'X = \sum_{i=1}^{n} x_i x_i'$ and $X'y = \sum_{i=1}^{n} x_i y_i$. So long as the matrix X has full rank (equal to K), OLS will produce estimates of the parameters. Note that this rank condition implies that $n \geq K$, so that there must be at least as many observations in the sample as parameters to be estimated. This is a remarkable property of estimation by OLS: it means that by applying the method to a linear relationship we generally get an estimate of each of the parameters of interest. The key concern in applied econometrics is whether these estimates are reliable or not.

The quality of the estimates depends on the specification of the model and in particular the stochastic specification. The basic assumptions of the latter are that:

(1) the explanatory variables and the error term are uncorrelated and
(2) the error term is independently and identically distributed with zero mean and constant variance of σ^2, summarized as $u_i \sim iid\left(0,\ \sigma^2\right)$.[2]

Writing the linear model for all n observations taken together as $y = X\beta + u$ (where u is the vector containing the n error terms), replacing y in the

[2] If the error term is assumed to be $u_i \sim N\left(0,\ \sigma^2\right)$, then the OLS estimator is also the maximum likelihood estimator.

definition the OLS estimator and taking expectations, reveals that under these conditions, the OLS estimator is unbiased:

$$E\left(\hat{\beta}\right) = \beta + E\left((X'X)^{-1} X'u\right) = \beta$$

The expectation in the second equality will be zero if there is no correlation between the explanatory variables and the error term. The variance–covariance matrix of the OLS estimator is given by:

$$\text{var}\left(\hat{\beta}\right) = \sigma^2 (X'X)^{-1}$$

The diagonal terms of this matrix are the variances of each of the estimated parameters:

$$\text{var}\left(\hat{\beta}_1\right), \ \text{var}\left(\hat{\beta}_2\right), \ldots, \text{var}\left(\hat{\beta}_K\right)$$

If X is non stochastic and the error term *iid*, the OLS estimator is the *best linear unbiased* estimator (or BLUE) of β in the sense that the variance of the OLS estimator is the smallest in the class of linear unbiased estimators. The 'best' epithet only requires assumption (2) to hold—since if X is non stochastic, it cannot be correlated with the error term. If X contains stochastic elements, then as long as there is no correlation between X and u, the OLS estimator is still unbiased. These are finite sample properties and therefore hold whatever the sample size (so long as $n \geq K$).

However, several useful statistical properties emerge as the number of observations in the sample gets larger and tends toward infinity. Given the increased availability of large-scale surveys, in practice these asymptotic properties may often be valid. In the context of OLS estimation if, in addition to (1), the probability limit *plim* $\left(\frac{X'X}{n}\right)$ is a positive definite matrix, then the OLS estimator is not only unbiased it is also consistent which means that:

$$plim\left(\hat{\beta}\right) = \beta + plim\left(\left(\frac{X'X}{n}\right)^{-1}\left(\frac{X'u}{n}\right)\right) = \beta$$

A useful way of thinking about consistency is in terms of the Chebyschev lemma which states that sufficient conditions for the estimator to be consistent are:

$$\lim_{n\to\infty} E\left(\hat{\beta}_k\right) = \beta_k \text{ and } \lim_{n\to\infty} \text{var}\left(\hat{\beta}_k\right) = 0 \text{ for } k = 1,\ 2,\ 3, \ldots,\ n$$

In other words, consistency requires the variance of the estimator to decline to zero asymptotically. Essentially, in order for the OLS estimator to be considered reliable, the term $(X'X)^{-1} X'u$ must either disappear on average (for unbiasedness) or disappear as the number of observations used gets large (for consistency).

If the OLS estimator is consistent, it also has an asymptotically normal distribution. This may seem odd in view of Tchebyschev's lemma since the asymptotic distribution of a consistent estimator would be degenerate (that is have a zero variance). What is meant by 'asymptotic distribution' is that *before* it degenerates, the distribution of the estimator will increasingly resemble a normal distribution as the sample size become larger. The interesting aspect of asymptotic properties is that there is no need to make strong assumptions about the nature of the error term. The downside is that these properties are only guaranteed to apply as the number of observations in the sample approaches infinity. We cannot be sure that they apply in a sample of 10,000 observations and it is even less certain when there are less than 1,000.

1.1.3 *Hypothesis Testing*

If the error term has a normal distribution, and the conditions are met in which the OLS estimator of β is unbiased, tests of null hypotheses can be undertaken using t tests and F tests in the standard way. These tests use the OLS parameter estimates and the OLS variance–covariance matrix $\text{var}\left(\hat{\beta}\right) = \sigma^2 \left(X'X\right)^{-1}$ with σ^2 replaced by its OLS estimate:

$$\hat{\sigma}^2 = \frac{1}{n-K}\sum_{i=1}^{n}\left(y_i - x_i'\hat{\beta}\right)^2$$

If one is confident with the assumption of the normal distribution of the error term then, since the OLS and maximum likelihood estimators of β are the same, likelihood ratio tests can be used—which is especially useful for testing nonlinear hypotheses (for example, $H_0 : \beta_2\beta_3 + \beta_4 = 0$). The hypothesis that the error term is normally distributed can be dispensed with in large samples since, as mentioned above, under certain regularity conditions asymptotically the OLS estimator has a normal distribution so that tests can be undertaken on the following basis:

(a) In order to test a null hypothesis on a single coefficient $H_0 : \beta_k = \beta_k^R$ we can use the t statistic:

$$t = \frac{\hat{\beta}_k - \beta_k^R}{\sqrt{\text{var}\left(\hat{\beta}_k\right)}} \underset{a}{\sim} N\left(0,\ 1\right)$$

(b) A composite hypothesis, such as $H_0 : \beta_2 = 1, \beta_4 = 0$, can be expressed for p linear restrictions, as $H_0 : R\beta = d$, where R is a $p \times K$ matrix of constants defining linear combinations of the elements of the vector β and d a $p \times 1$

vector of constants (in the example $p = 2$), we can use the F statistic when the OLS estimator is unbiased. The asymptotic form is given by:

$$p \times F = \left(R\hat{\beta} - d\right)' \left(R\,\mathrm{var}\left(\hat{\beta}\right)\,R'\right)^{-1} \left(R\hat{\beta} - d\right) \underset{a}{\sim} \chi_p^2$$

where F is the traditional 'F statistic'.[3] The same numerical value of this statistic can be obtained by running an OLS regression with the p linear restrictions imposed and comparing the residual sum of squares obtained (RSS^R) with that resulting from estimation without the restrictions (RSS^U):

$$p \times F = (n - K)\left(\frac{RSS^R - RSS^U}{RSS^U}\right) \underset{a}{\sim} \chi_p^2$$

These asymptotic forms of the t and F tests require the error term to be *iid* and uncorrelated with the explanatory variables. They are asymptotic tests and independent of distributional assumptions—it is not necessary to assume that the error term has a normal distribution as would be the case if we were to use statistics that had Student t and F distributions, respectively.

One issue that is sometimes raised in econometric analysis with large samples is the way in which the reduction in the variance of the estimator inflates these test statistics (see, for example, Deaton, 1996). It is has been suggested that instead of using critical values from the limiting distribution, we should use the Schwarz information criterion. For a null hypothesis with p restrictions, the F statistic is compared to $p\log(n)$ and for a single restriction the t statistic is compared to $\sqrt{\log(n)}$. For a t test with a sample size of 80,000, the critical value would be 3.36 instead of 1.96.

1.2 Specification Issues in the Linear Model

Given that the properties of the OLS estimator as well as the different tests are derived from the way the model is constructed, including the stochastic specification of the model, it is important to undertake diagnostic checks. This is achieved by using misspecification tests and where these indicate that there is a problem there is often an alternative approach available, through either an alternative estimator or a corrective transformation. In cross-section analysis there has traditionally been relatively little interest in the issue of error autocorrelation, since it should not be present in samples that are supposed be drawn randomly from a population at a given moment in time.[4] There may be correlation created when data from different levels

[3] The traditional F statistic is obtained by dividing through by the number of restrictions (p).

[4] There may be spatial autocorrelation if people in the same neighbourhoods are influenced by common unobserved factors, or if there is 'keeping up with the Jones' type behaviour.

are combined—for example using regional variables in an equation estimated for individuals (this is treated below in Chapter 2). More prevalent in cross-section analysis is the presence of unobserved heterogeneity which can give rise to two econometric problems—heteroscedasticity and correlation between the error term and the explanatory variables. It should be emphasized that the former is not as serious as the latter. The misspecification of the relationship between the dependent and explanatory variables can also seriously undermine the reliability of the estimates. We describe these different problem areas, and present tools for diagnosing the problems and methods for solving or avoiding them.

1.2.1 *Heteroscedasticity*

Heteroscedasticity entails the failure of the 'identical' part of the *iid* specification of the error term. It means that the variance of the error term changes from one observation to another, often in relation to a variable—for example, $\text{var}(u_i) = \sigma^2 z_i$. If it is the sole problem with the model,[5] it has no consequences for the unbiasedness property of the OLS estimator, but it does affect the way in which the variance of the estimator is calculated and thus will cause bias in the test statistics. If the source of the heteroscedasticity is known, the linear relation can be transformed and the generalized least squares estimates be obtained. In the presence of heteroscedasticity, the GLS estimator has a smaller variance than OLS. However, in practice it is rare to have information on the specific form of heteroscedasticity, and an alternative strategy is to estimate the variance of the OLS estimator using a more appropriate formula. Halbert White (1980) has proposed the following means of obtaining a consistent estimate of the variance covariance matrix of the OLS estimator in the presence of heteroscedasticity:[6]

$$\text{var}\left(\hat{\beta}\right) = (X'X)^{-1}\left(\sum_{i=1}^{n} \hat{u}_i^2 x_i x_i'\right)(X'X)^{-1}$$

where $\hat{u}_i = y_i - x_i'\hat{\beta}$ is the regression residual for observation i. In most modern empirical analysis in labour economics, authors directly present 'heteroscedasticity-consistent standard errors'[7] which are simply the square roots of the diagonal elements of this matrix.

The presence of heteroscedasticity can be diagnosed using the White test (which White presented in the same article as the method for the consistent

5 Heteroscedasticity is sometimes detected where the actual relationship is nonlinear or where a key variable has been omitted.

6 This is sometimes referred to a 'sandwich' estimator.

7 These are also called robust standard errors or White standard errors. Using White standard errors is sometimes called 'whitewashing'!

estimation of the matrix), which is performed, as with many misspecification tests, in two steps:

(1) obtain the OLS residuals $\hat{u}_i = y_i - x_i'\hat{\beta}$

(2) regress $\hat{u}_i^2$ on the $p = \frac{1}{2}k(k+1)$ unique elements in the matrix $x_i x_i'$ (and include a constant if there is none in x_i'). Using the R^2 from this regression, calculate the statistic $H = nR^2$ which is distributed as χ_p^2 under the null (that is if H is greater than critical value the hypothesis is rejected).

1.2.2 *Correlation Between Explanatory Variables and the error term*

A more serious problem occurs if there is correlation between the error term and any of the explanatory variables. This may happen if one or more of the latter are subject to measurement error. More commonly the correlation is due to the endogeneity of the explanatory variables or regressors. In this case, the OLS estimator is both biased and inconsistent (the extent of the bias could even be such that the sign of a coefficient is reversed). A useful way of seeing why this is the case is by recalling how the OLS estimator is obtained. Minimizing the sum of squared residuals gives rise to a set of first order conditions (see the Appendix) in which the residual is orthogonal to—and therefore uncorrelated with—each regressor:

$$\sum_{i=1}^{n} \hat{u}_i x_{1i} = 0, \sum_{i=1}^{n} \hat{u}_i x_{2i} = 0 \text{ ,...., } \sum_{i=1}^{n} \hat{u}_i x_{Ki} = 0$$

However, the residual $\hat{u}_i = y_i - x_i'\hat{\beta}$ is just an estimate of the error term, $u_i = y_i - x_i'\beta$. OLS estimation of the parameter vector β forces this orthogonality between the regressors and the residual. Therefore OLS estimates will diverge on average and asymptotically from the population values of the parameters if the error term u_i is correlated with (that is is not orthogonal to) any of the regressors $x_{1i}, x_{2i}, \ldots x_{Ki}$—and so will be biased and inconsistent.

In order to deal with this case, an alternative estimation strategy will be necessary. However, *when the explanatory variable is correlated with the error term, no estimator is unbiased.* The most that can be obtained are consistent estimates, and this involves using data on one or more variables from *outside* the sample used for calculating the OLS estimates of the parameters of interest. One possible avenue is available if the process that determines the endogenous regressor is known (from a theoretical point of view) in which case a second equation can be specified for this variable and a 'simultaneous equations' approach can be adopted. This requires that an a priori distinction be made between endogenous and exogenous variables, with as many equations in the system as there are endogenous variables, along with special attention being paid to the question of identification.

While such an approach is feasible in cases where there is a strong theoretical basis for analysis, in most labour economics applications the endogeneity tends to be more a matter of suspicion (be it illusory or real), rather than the prediction of some theoretical model. Practitioners generally adopt the shortcut of using *instrumental variables* rather than specifying a precise multi-equation structural model. In terms of the terminology of simultaneous equations, an instrumental variable is an exogenous variable which plays a role in the determination of the endogenous regressor. In terms of the application of the instrumental variables estimator, the instruments are required to have the dual property of being correlated with the suspected regressor but not correlated with the error term. In other words, the only way an instrumental variable can have an effect on the dependent variable is *indirectly*; only through its effect on the endogenous regressor.

In order to see what is obtained from applying the instrumental variables technique, consider the simple bivariate case:[8]

$$y_i = z_i \alpha + u_i$$

Endogeneity of z_i in the sense that it is correlated with u_i means that

$$plim \frac{\sum_{i=1}^{n} z_i u_i}{n} \neq 0$$

The OLS estimator is biased ($E(\hat{\alpha}) \neq \alpha$) and more importantly inconsistent ($plim\ \hat{\alpha} \neq \alpha$) since:

$$plim\ \hat{\alpha} = \alpha + \frac{plim \frac{\sum_{i=1}^{n} z_i u_i}{n}}{plim \frac{\sum_{i=1}^{n} z_i^2}{n}} \neq 0$$

The method of instrumental variables (IV) enables consistent estimates to be obtained by 'correcting' the problem created by the correlation between z_i and u_i. The instrument—call it w_i—must be correlated with z_i but not with u_i. The IV estimator of α is given by:

$$\tilde{\alpha}_V = \frac{\sum_{i=1}^{n} w_i y_i}{\sum_{i=1}^{n} w_i z_i}$$

[8] These results generalize to the case of several explanatory variables and more than one endogenous regressor.

Replacing y_i in this formula and taking probability limits yields:

$$plim\ \tilde{\alpha}_V = \alpha + \frac{plim\left(\sum_{i=1}^{n} w_i u_i \Big/ n\right)}{plim\left(\sum_{i=1}^{n} w_i z_i \Big/ n\right)}$$

If the denominator is defined (and not equal to zero), the absence of correlation between the instrument and the error term means that the IV estimator is consistent:

$$plim\ \frac{\sum_{i=1}^{n} w_i u_i}{n} = 0, \quad \text{and} \quad plim\ \tilde{\alpha}_V = \alpha + \frac{0}{plim\left(\sum_{i=1}^{n} w_i z_i \Big/ n\right)} = \alpha$$

It has already been mentioned that, in labour economics, the presence of endogenous regressors and the existence of correlation between regressors and the error term is often due to suspicions on the part of the economist rather than derived from rigorous theoretical reasoning. It would be preferable therefore to test to see if these suspicions are well-founded rather than simply proceed on the basis that they are real. A test that examines whether OLS estimates are biased because of correlation between regressor and error term has been proposed by Jerry Hausman (1978). The idea behind the test is that if there is no correlation between regressor and error term, the OLS and IV estimators are both consistent. If there is a correlation, then the IV estimator is still consistent whereas the OLS is not. Any significant divergence between the two therefore indicates the presence of a correlation between regressor and error term. A straightforward version of his test is in two steps (see, for example, Davidson and MacKinnon, 1993, for a derivation):

(1) obtain the OLS residuals $\hat{v}_i$ of the regression of z_i on w_i: $z_i = w_i\hat{\gamma} + \hat{v}_i$
(2) run a regression of y_i on z_i and $\hat{v}_i$[9]: $y_i = z_i\alpha + \hat{v}_i\phi + \varepsilon_i$.

The Hausman test is of the null hypothesis: $H_0 : \phi = 0$, which is simply a t test. Being an asymptotic test, the 5% critical value is 1.96 since it is obtained from the standard normal distribution. Like the IV estimator itself, the reliability of the Hausman test depends on the quality of the instruments used.

The above reasoning is for the case where a single instrumental variable is used for a single endogenous explanatory variable. In fact, it is possible

[9] In fact the test produces the same result if $\hat{v}_i$ is replaced by $\hat{z}_i = w_i\hat{\gamma}$.

to use more than one instrument per endogenous regressor. Consider the following relation with two explanatory variables:

$$y_i = \beta_1 + \beta_2 x_{2i} + \beta_3 x_{3i} + u_i$$

It is thought that explanatory variable x_{2i} is correlated with the error term u_i while x_{3i} is above suspicion (and therefore not correlated with u_i). In order to obtain consistent estimates, two instrumental variables are available: w_{1i} and w_{2i}. In this case, the easiest way of describing how to obtain IV estimates of the parameters of interest is through the application of the *two stage least squares* procedure. In the first stage, the suspected variable x_{2i} is regressed on both the instrumental variables and any exogenous variables that appear in the equation we are interested in (in this case, the constant and x_{3i}). The first stage regression is therefore:

$$x_{2i} = \gamma_0 + \gamma_1 w_{1i} + \gamma_2 w_{2i} + \gamma_3 x_{3i} + v_i$$

The parameters of this equation are estimated by OLS and the fitted value of x_{2i} ($\hat{x}_{2i}$) from this first stage is used as a replacement for the actual value of x_{2i} in the equation for y_i:

$$y_i = \beta_1 + \beta_2 \hat{x}_{2i} + \beta_3 x_{3i} + \varepsilon_i$$

where the fitted value $\hat{x}_{2i}$ is given by $\hat{x}_{2i} = \hat{\gamma}_0 + \hat{\gamma}_1 w_{1i} + \hat{\gamma}_2 w_{2i} + \hat{\gamma}_3 x_{3i}$ and ε_i is the error term now that $\hat{x}_{2i}$ has replaced x_{2i}. In this second stage, the parameters are estimated by OLS and the resulting estimator is called the two stage least squares (2SLS) estimator.

Two stage least squares is an instrumental variables estimator[10] and the double application of OLS is simply a method for calculating the values of the parameters. The same numerical values could have been obtained by the single, direct application of an IV matrix formula. It is important to remember that the (unknown) population parameters in the original equation and the transformed equation are the same. Two stage least squares (or instrumental variables) is just a different method for estimating the same parameters of interest in a given linear model. OLS is thought to give biased and inconsistent estimates of the βs and instrumental variables/2SLS provides consistent, though still biased, estimates.

Presenting the IV estimator in this two stage framework provides a very intuitive way of obtaining reliable estimates. The fitted value from the first stage is a linear combination of variables that are by definition not correlated with u_i, the error term in the original equation. Replacing x_{2i} by its fitted

[10] In fact it called the Generalized Instrumental Variables Estimator (GIVE) when there are more instruments than endogenous regressors.

value removes the correlation between the error term in the second stage (ε_i) and the explanatory variables in the equation. Furthermore, the first stage regression picks up the correlation between the explanatory variable and the instrumental variables. Thus the two requirements for admissible instruments are met.

One immediate disadvantage with the two stage least squares approach (compared to the direct application of instrumental variables) is that the OLS estimated standard errors in the second stage are not the relevant ones. These have to be estimated using the sum of squared IV residuals, where the IV residual is given by:

$$\tilde{\varepsilon}_{iV} = y_i - \left(\tilde{\beta}_{1V} + \tilde{\beta}_{2V}\, x_{2i} + \tilde{\beta}_{1V}\, x_{3i}\right)$$

IV and 2SLS are all very well in theory as a solution to a problem encountered with OLS estimation. There are, however, a number of important features of IV estimation that mean that it should be used with due care and attention. First, the IV estimator is not an unbiased estimator when a regressor is correlated with the error term, and so it may not be appropriate to have more confidence in instrumental variables than OLS when the sample size is small. The same applies to the variance of the IV estimator, which is an asymptotic derivation and thus valid for large samples. Hypothesis tests using IV estimates are therefore based on an asymptotic (normal) distribution which may not always be reliable. Secondly, there is no foolproof method for choosing the instruments. Ad hoc reasoning and rules of thumb rather than theoretical rigour tend to be used in practice and a bad choice of instrument means that it may not improve on OLS estimation. A major requirement is the absence of correlation of the instrument with the error term of the equation of interest, and there is currently no scientific method of selecting variables that have this property with a high degree of certainty.

When there is one suspicious explanatory variable and more than one instrumental variable available, a test of the validity of the instrumental variables is possible.[11] This consists in estimating the following regression:

$$\tilde{\varepsilon}_{iV} = \lambda_1 w_{1i} + \lambda_2 w_{2i} + \lambda_3 x_{3i} + v_i$$

that is a regression of the IV residual on the two instruments and any exogenous explanatory variables but no constant, and using the (uncentred) R^2 from this regression to calculate the test statistic $S = n \times R^2$. If this statistic is smaller than the chi square critical value for 1 degree of freedom ($\chi_1^2 = 3.84$ at the 5% level), then the instruments can be regarded as valid. Essentially,

[11] This is sometimes referred to as the 'Sargan test' after Sargan (1964).

this test examines whether there is any correlation between the equation residual and one of the instruments. This correlation should be zero if the instruments possess their defining property. Note that this test is only capable of detecting instrument validity when there are more instruments than suspicious regressors, and only really tests the validity of the 'redundant' instruments (if there are p instruments used, the degrees of freedom in the test are equal to $p - 1$). In other words, it is only applicable for over-identifying instruments, and for this reason it is sometimes referred to as an *over-identification test*. Furthermore, it hinges on there being at least one valid instrument.

A third issue, and linked to the previous point, is that there is a growing literature on the problems of 'weak' instruments, in which the chosen instrument is weakly correlated with the endogenous regressor (see Stock et al., 2002, for a survey). This concerns the first requirement of an instrumental variable and, if the correlation is low, the IV estimator can be very biased. One simple test that can be undertaken is whether the coefficients on the instruments (γ_1 and γ_2) are zero in the first stage regression:

$$x_{2i} = \gamma_0 + \gamma_1 w_{1i} + \gamma_2 w_{2i} + \gamma_3 x_{3i} + v_i$$

This involves calculating the standard F test statistic for the hypothesis $H_0 : \gamma_1 = \gamma_2 = 0$. It is suggested that this statistic should be greater than ten for the instruments to be valid. If it is less than five, the weakness of the instruments could cause substantial bias. Another paper, by Stock and Yogo (2002), suggests that even these values are too low, and for one problematic regressor the F statistic should be greater than 20 (and higher still when there are several potentially endogenous regressors).

The issue of correlation between explanatory variables and the error term is one of the major concerns in applied econometrics. It must always be borne in mind since nearly all the data used are generated by economic and social behaviour, rather than controlled experiments in a research laboratory. Nearly all variables used in labour economics applications are endogenous in some sense—exceptions are age and physical characteristics such as height. What is important in econometrics is whether the endogeneity is relevant for the estimation of the parameters of interest, and in a linear model this is equivalent to establishing whether the explanatory variables are correlated with the error term. The potential endogeneity of a variable is determined either by recourse to a theoretical model or by some less rigorous form of reasoning. It is has been emphasized that in the main it emanates from suspicion. In order to examine this suspicion, practitioners seek instrumental variables—variables that do not appear in their model and that have the dual property of being correlated with the suspected explanatory variable but not correlated with the error term. In large samples, if the instrumental variable is 'valid' and 'not weak', reliable estimates can be obtained. In small samples, it is difficult to say whether IV estimates improve upon OLS.

If an instrumental variable is used, a series of tests can be undertaken to see whether (a) there is any difference between the IV and OLS estimates—a Hausman test; (b) an F test to see whether the instrument is weak; and (c) in the case where there is more than one instrumental variable per suspected regressor, an over-identifying instruments test. Sometimes it is not possible to proceed with instrumental variables estimation at all—either because there are none available in the data set or because no variable in the data set has the required properties. In these circumstances, it will be necessary to interpret the results with caution and attempt to assess the direction of any bias.

1.2.3 *Misspecification of the Systematic Component*

A final set of specification issues related to linear regression concerns the systematic component $x_i'\beta$. This can be misspecified in two ways. First, it is possible that important explanatory variables have been omitted and, second, the relation between x_i and y_i may not be linear. The first of these is a standard problem and it is difficult to gauge its importance—although the RESET test may be helpful (see below). It can cause OLS estimates to be biased through the usual mechanism of a non-zero correlation between included regressors and the error term, since any relevant variable excluded from the systematic component will be found in the error term. If a group of variables represented by the matrix Z is wrongly omitted from the regression so that (a) $y = X\beta + u$ is estimated instead of (b) $y = X\beta + Z\gamma + v$, then the extent of the bias in the estimation of β in the former depends in part on the degree of correlation between the included and the excluded regressors. Replacing y as defined in (b) in the definition of the OLS estimator $\hat{\beta} = (X'X)^{-1}X'y$ and taking expectations:

$$E\left(\hat{\beta}\right) = \beta + E\left((X'X)^{-1}X'Z\gamma\right) \equiv \beta + E\left(\hat{\pi}\right)\gamma = \beta + \pi\gamma$$

where $\hat{\pi} = (X'X)^{-1}X'Z$. If X and Z are uncorrelated then $E\left(\hat{\pi}\right) = \{0\}$, and there is no bias.

However, two guidelines are available to practitioners. First, if X and Z are correlated and the signs of the parameters in the vector γ can be determined from theory or intuition, the direction of the bias can be determined. A second guideline is that including redundant regressors will not create bias in the parameter estimates, but will increase the variance of the OLS estimator.

It is therefore advisable to retain such regressors and test the null hypothesis that their coefficients are jointly zero rather than exclude them on the basis of theoretical or a priori reasoning. Many practitioners simply over-specify the model and err on the side of caution. While this involves an efficiency loss (that is a higher variance of the estimator), this loss will be small in large samples.

Problems can also arise if the relation between the dependent and explanatory variables is not linear. Least squares estimation requires *linearity in the parameters*, so nonlinear relations, such as standard polynomial functions or where some or all of the variables are expressed in logarithms that satisfy this condition, can still be treated as 'linear' models. If the relationship is nonlinear in the parameters, then maximum likelihood estimation is possible if one is prepared to introduce a restrictive distributional assumption, though this will require the use of an iterative estimation technique. Before embarking on this route, the RESET test proposed by J.B. Ramsey (1969) can be used to diagnose the presence of nonlinearities. This, as with so many specification tests, is implemented in two steps:

(1) obtain the OLS fitted values $\hat{y}_i = x_i'\hat{\beta}$ from the regression $y_i = x_i'\beta + u_i$,
(2) run the following regression $y_i = \psi\ \hat{y}_i^2 + x_i'\beta + \varepsilon_i$.

The RESET test is of the null hypothesis $H_0 : \psi = 0$, and is a simple t test. If it is thought appropriate, higher polynomial terms in $\hat{y}_i$ can be included ($\psi\ \hat{y}_i^2$ is replaced by $\psi_1\ \hat{y}_i^2 + \psi_2\ \hat{y}_i^3 + \psi_3\ \hat{y}_i^4 \ldots.$) and the resulting test is an F test of all such terms having zero coefficients $H_0 : \psi_1 = \psi_2 = \psi_3 = \ldots = 0$. If the null hypothesis is not rejected, then the linear specification is admissible. On the other hand, rejection can be the result of nonlinearities in the relationship between y_i and x_i, or the omission of one or more important explanatory variables. If it is concluded that the relationship is nonlinear then either an alternative estimation approach is adopted, such as maximum likelihood, or the relationship is transformed in a way that renders it nonlinear in the variables but linear in the parameters (for example, transforming the variables into logarithms, so long as all the variables in question take strictly positive values).

In certain cases an underlying theoretical model is informative about the functional form—as in the Mincer equation. Failing this, looking at the data can sometimes help. For example, if the density of the dependent variable is skewed to the right as in Fig. 1.1, transforming into logarithms will produce an approximately symmetric and possibly normal distribution. Obviously a logarithmic transformation only applies to positively valued variables. Scatter plots and non parametric methods can also assist in the choice of functional form.

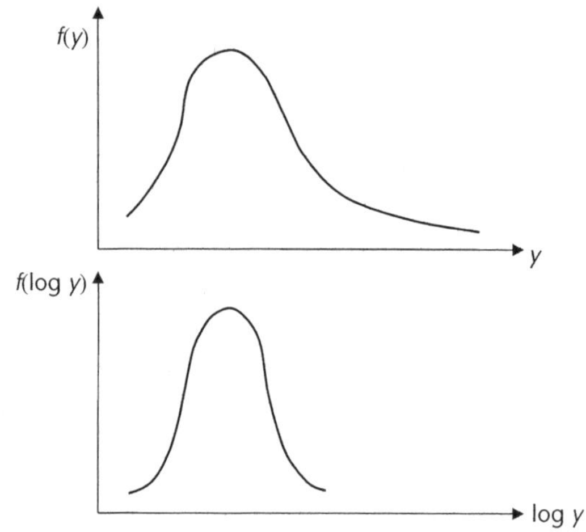

Figure 1.1. Densities of a skewed and log-transformed variable

1.3 Using the Linear Regression Model in Labour Economics—The Mincer Earnings Equation

The standard Mincer (1974) earnings equation relates the log of hourly earnings ($\log w_i$) to years of education (s_i) and a quadratic function of labour market experience (ex_i) in a linear fashion:

$$\log w_i = \alpha + \beta\, s_i + \gamma_1 ex_i + \gamma_2 ex_i^2 + u_i$$

The relation is linear in the parameters and so least squares estimation is applicable. The counter-factual interpretation is that two individuals (i and j), who are in all respects identical except that one has a year's more schooling, will have different wages where the log of the difference is:

$$\log w_i - \log w_j = \beta$$

$$\text{and } \log\, w_i - \log\, w_j = \log\left(\frac{w_i}{w_j}\right) \Rightarrow \frac{w_i - w_j}{w_j} = \exp(\beta) - 1$$

The latter is the *proportional difference in earnings* as a result of having one year more of education. It is also referred to as the rate of return to an additional year of education. Note that when β is small ($\beta < 0.1$) the following approximation holds: $\exp(\beta) - 1 \approx \beta$, in which case β is roughly the return to education. However, this approximation should probably be avoided as a general rule (Table 1.1 shows the accuracy of the approximation).

The interpretation of the effect of labour market experience is not so straightforward since the slope of the earnings function varies with

Table 1.1. Calculation of the return to education

Value of coefficient β	Proportionate return to education $\theta = \exp(\beta) - 1$
0.02	0.020
0.05	0.051
0.08	0.083
0.10	0.105
0.15	0.162
0.20	0.221
0.30	0.350
0.50	0.649

experience. For a given level of education and unobserved characteristics (u), the slope of the earnings function is:

$$\frac{\partial \log w_i}{\partial ex_i} = \gamma_1 + 2\gamma_2 ex_i$$

If $\gamma_1 > 0, \gamma_2 < 0_i$, the quadratic log earnings–experience relation is concave and the slope will at some point will become negative (after a level of experience equal of $ex^* = -\frac{\gamma_1}{2\gamma_2}$).

1.3.1 *Variable Definitions*

While estimation of the parameters is straightforward, there are often problems with the correspondence between the variables as defined in the theoretical framework and the observed counterpart in cross-section household surveys. These problems concern each of the three variables that figure in the earnings equation. First, a precise measure of hourly earnings is difficult to obtain for a large part of the workforce which doesn't have contractually defined hours. Furthermore, hourly earnings are often derived from weekly or monthly earnings for the time period prior to interview for a survey: 'what was your last monthly earnings?'; 'how many hours did you work last week/month?'. In the Current Population Survey, for example, only those in the outgoing rotation group are asked to specify 'usual hourly earnings'. In many occupations hourly earnings are not meaningful because payment is for a number of tasks or by results. Second, the Mincer approach treats investment in education in terms of the purchase of an extra year's education. This measure of education is problematic in countries where it is the diploma or qualification that counts and not the number of years. In France, for example, where re-taking the same year is very frequent (more than 50% re-take a year in some disciplines), the person who has the highest number of years of education is probably the one who is the least able. Third, there is a divergence between labour market experience and the number of years since the individual left full-time education, due to periods of unemployment and periods out of the labour force. It is usual to refer to 'potential' experience (current age minus age at the end of full-time education) and recognize that it is being used as a proxy. Note that this means that any problems with the education variable (such as endogeneity—see below) will also be present in the experience variable.

1.3.2 *Specification Issues in the Earnings Equation*

THE EDUCATION VARIABLE

Apart from these issues of definition and measurement, the actual specification of the equation can be questioned. Linked to the question of years of education or diploma obtained, it is common to use dummy variables to represent an individual's education level. For example if there are four education levels: (1) less than high school; (2) high school graduate; (3) bachelor's degree; and (4) a higher degree, then four dummy variables can be defined as follows:

Highest education level obtained		Otherwise
Less than high school	$d_{1i} = 1$	$d_{1i} = 0$
High school only	$d_{2i} = 1$	$d_{2i} = 0$
Bachelor's degree only	$d_{3i} = 1$	$d_{3i} = 0$
Higher degree	$d_{4i} = 1$	$d_{4i} = 0$

Only one of these dummy variables is non-zero for each individual. These variables replace the education variable in the earnings equation:

$$\log w_i = \alpha\, e_i + \beta_1 d_{1i} + \beta_2 d_{2i} + \beta_3 d_{3i} + \beta_4 d_{4i} + \gamma_1 ex_i + \gamma_2 ex_i^2 + u_i$$

where $e_i = 1$ for all i. However, this representation of education level means that the constant cannot be identified because of perfect multi-collinearity between the dummy variables and e_i. In the terminology used above, the rank of the X matrix will be less than the number of parameters to be estimated. It is customary to define a reference level of education and exclude the dummy variable for that level. For example, if less than high school is the reference then the following equation is estimated:

$$\log w_i = \alpha_1 + \beta_2 d_{2i} + \beta_3 d_{3i} + \beta_4 d_{4i} + \gamma_1 ex_i + \gamma_2 ex_i^2 + u_i$$

Note that the constant term is now given by $\alpha_1 = \alpha + \beta_1$. The constant α itself is not identified, and the other coefficients are interpreted with reference to a counter-factual consisting of an individual who has a less than high school education level. Thus an individual with a bachelor's degree will earn proportionally $\exp(\beta_3) - 1$ more than an individual with the same experience and same unobserved characteristics but who has not finished high school. An individual with a master's degree will earn $\exp(\beta_4 - \beta_3) - 1$ more, proportionally, than an identical individual who has a bachelor's degree. This approach would be suitable for the French education system mentioned above.

THE EXPERIENCE–EARNINGS RELATIONSHIP

A second specification issue that has been addressed in econometric studies of earnings is the shape of the earnings–experience profile. The quadratic form is the one proposed by Mincer on the basis of assumptions about investment in post-school training and human capital depreciation. However, this particular form restricts the shape of the profile to be symmetric about the maximum. For example, a RESET test suggests that the relationship is misspecified (RESET $t = 3.51$). Many modern studies use either (a) a higher order polynomial—possibly up to the 4th degree—or (b) a step function defined using dummy variables or (c) a spline function.

(a) A higher order polynomial enables the symmetry imposed by the quadratic specification to be avoided. It also means that the experience–earnings profile is less likely to reach a maximum before retirement age. For example, in the quartic specification:

$$\log w_i = \alpha + \beta s_i + \gamma_1 ex_i + \gamma_2 ex_i^2 + \gamma_3 ex_i^3 + \gamma_4 ex_i^4 + u_i$$

The marginal effect (on log earnings) of one more year of experience is:

$$\frac{\partial \log w_i}{\partial \, ex_i} = \gamma_1 + 2\gamma_2 ex_i + 3\gamma_3 ex_i^2 + 4\gamma_4 ex_i^3$$

For the same sample used above the OLS estimates are:

$$\log w_i = 0.84 + 0.075\ s_i + 0.075\ ex_i - 0.0036\ ex_i^2 + 0.00008\ ex_i^3 - (0.7 \times 10^{-6})\ ex_i^4 + \hat{u}_i$$

Standard errors are not presented since all t statistics are greater than 70 in absolute value. However the RESET test suggests that this specification is not adequate (RESET $t = 2.51$). One problem that needs to be recognized is that the polynomial is a local approximation to a nonlinear function, and therefore valid *locally*—that is, for values of the variable 'experience' in the support (that is the range of values in the data set). It would be unwise to use the estimates obtained from such a specification to extrapolate outside the support. For example, because of the tendency in many countries for labour market participation rates to decline after the age of 55, many studies of earnings differences simply truncate the sample at age of 54. A second issue is that adding higher order terms to a basic quadratic equation will alter the

Table 1.2. The earnings experience relationship in the United States

	Coefficient	Standard error
Constant	0.83	0.015
Education	0.076	0.0007
Experience	0.081	0.008
Experience^2	−0.0045	0.0017
Experience^3	0.00019(ns)	0.00035
Experience^4	-0.6×10^{-7}(ns)	0.7×10^{-6}
Experience^5	-0.4×10^{-8}(ns)	0.2×10^{-7}
Experience^6	-0.6×10^{-10}(ns)	0.1×10^{-9}

ns – not significant at 5%

form of the function within the support. Some of the higher order terms may have insignificant coefficients, and removing them may be justified at first sight. However, in this context, it is important to undertake F tests of the *joint* significance of the higher order terms. In the above example, if 5th and 6th order polynomials are added, the results obtained are presented in Table 1.2.

On the basis of individual t statistics, the only significant terms are the first two, so that the quadratic specification would at first sight appear adequate. However an F test of the joint hypothesis that the coefficients of the four variables Experience^3 to Experience^6 are zero clearly rejects the null ($F(4, 80193) = 105.5$, $p = 0.000$). The restrictions justifying the removal of only Experience^5 and Experience^6 are not rejected ($F(2, 80193) = 2.56$, $p = 0{,}08$).

(b) An alternative representation of a nonlinear profile is to use a step function where the experience variable is partitioned into intervals and a dummy variable defined for each interval (dex_{2i}). If there are, say, four such intervals (0–10, 11–20, 21–30, 31–40) the earnings regression can be written as

$$\log w_i = \alpha_1 + \beta\, s_i + \gamma_2 dex_{2i} + \gamma_3 dex_{3i} + \gamma_4 dex_{4i} + u_i$$

where the first interval is the reference category and is incorporated in the constant term (see the education dummy example above). The effect of experience can only be interpreted in a counter-factual sense since earnings are no longer a continuous function of experience and so the marginal effect is undefined. Take two otherwise identical individuals, one of whom has 15 years experience ($dex_{2i} = 1$) and the other 5 years ($dex_{2i} = 0$). The difference in log earnings will be γ_2 and the former will earn $(\exp(\gamma_2) - 1) \times 100\%$ more than the latter. For the sample used this difference is estimated to be 31.5% since

$$\log w_i = 1.12 + 0.075\; s_i + 0.274\; dex_{2i} + 0.339\; dex_{3i} + 0.351\; dex_{4i} + \hat{u}_i$$

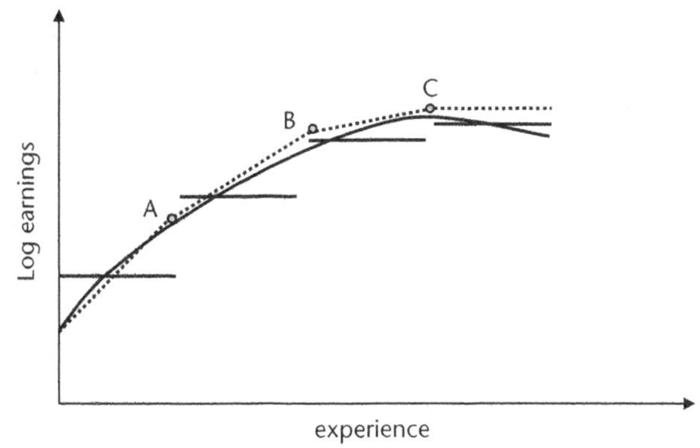

Figure 1.2. Different specifications of the experience–earnings profile

All t statistics are greater than 7.5 in absolute value except for the coefficient γ_4 ($t = -5.0$), although the RESET test rejects this specification (RESET $t = 3.83$). A major weakness with this approach and the next is that the issue of defining meaningful intervals has to be dealt with.

(c) In between the two previous approaches lies the notion of a spline function in which the earnings–experience relationship is specified as being piece-wise linear. This is illustrated along with the previous approaches to modelling earnings–experience profiles in Fig. 1.2. The difference compared with the step function approach is that the marginal rate of return is fixed within an interval and allowed to vary between intervals. Pursuing the previous example, in the 0 to 10 year interval, the return to an extra year's experience is γ_1, in the interval 11 to 20 the marginal return is γ_2, and so forth. This gives rise to piece-wise linear function.

In order for the segments to join up at the 'knots' (A, B, and C in Fig. 1.2), the spline function is specified as follows. Define the dummy variables:

$$\delta_2 = 1 \text{ if } ex_i > 10 \text{ otherwise } \delta_2 = 0$$

$$\delta_3 = 1 \text{ if } ex_i > 20 \text{ otherwise } \delta_3 = 0$$

$$\delta_4 = 1 \text{ if } ex_i > 30 \text{ otherwise } \delta_4 = 0$$

and estimate the parameters of the regression:

$$\log w_i = \alpha_1 + \beta\, s_i + \gamma_1 ex_i + \gamma_2^* \left[\delta_2 \left(ex_i - 10\right)\right] + \gamma_3^* \left[\delta_3 \left(ex_i - 20\right)\right] + \gamma_4^* \left[\delta_4 \left(ex_i - 30\right)\right] + u_i$$

This involves creating the variables $[\delta_2\,(ex_i - 10)]$, $[\delta_3\,(ex_i - 20)]$, $[\delta_4\,(ex_i - 30)]$ and including these in the place of the polynomial terms in experience. The marginal effect of a year's extra experience rises from γ_1 to $\gamma_1 + \gamma_2^*$ after 10 years experience, to $\gamma_1 + \gamma_2^* + \gamma_3^*$ after 20 years, and $\gamma_1 + \gamma_2^* + \gamma_3^* + \gamma_4^*$ after 30 years. The estimated earnings equation is:

$$\log w_i = 0.89 + 0.075\ s_i + 0.043\ ex_i - 0.032\ [\delta_2\,(ex_i - 10)]$$
$$-0.009\ [\delta_3\,(ex_i - 20)] - 0.0022\ [\delta_4\,(ex_i - 30)] + \hat{u}_i$$

All t statistics are greater than 8 in absolute value except that of γ_4, which is not significant, and the RESET test suggests that the specification is adequate (RESET $t = 1.53$).

THE ENDOGENEITY OF EDUCATION

A final specification issue in the Mincer earnings equation[12] arises because the equation presented here is derived from a theoretical human capital model and has a special interpretation. The basic hypothesis is that there are no constraints preventing an individual from choosing his/her optimal level of educational investment—that is there are no effects of family background, intellectual ability, unequal access to borrowing, and so forth. If there are unobserved factors that affect both education and earnings, then the estimated rate of return to education will be biased upwards due to the correlation between the explanatory variable and the error term. For example, Paul Taubman's (1976) work using data on twins shows in a dramatic way how the estimated rate of return is reduced by half when the fact that the two people are twins is used in estimation rather than treating them as two individuals selected at random.

An asymptotic approach to reducing bias in the estimation of returns to education due to background and ability is to use the method of instrumental variables, with say father's education (f_i) as an instrument. Given that there are several variables in the equation, the two stage least squares version of instrumental variables estimation is easier to implement and comprehend. This would proceed as follows. In order to obtain consistent estimates of the parameter β in the following regression:

$$\log w_i = \alpha + \beta\ s_i + \gamma_1 ex_i + \gamma_2 ex_i^2 + u_i$$

(i) regress s_i on the instrument f_i and ex_i, ex_i^2 (the latter two variables serve as instruments 'for themselves'),

[12] Other influences on earnings (institutional factors, imperfections, incentive mechanisms ...) are not formally part of the Mincer equation. The estimated returns to human capital may be biased because of these omitted factors, but then the processes that generate earnings differences are not those modelled by the Mincer equation as derived from Mincer's theoretical model.

(ii) take the fitted value of education from the first stage: $\hat{s}_i = \hat{\gamma}_0 + \hat{\gamma}_1 f_i + \hat{\gamma}_2 ex_i + \hat{\gamma}_3 ex_i^2$ and replace s_i by $\hat{s}_i$ in the earnings equation:

$$\log w_i = \alpha + \beta\ \hat{s}_i + \gamma_1 ex_i + \gamma_2 ex_i^2 + \varepsilon_i$$

Note the change of error term. Applying OLS to this equation provides IV estimates of the parameters, and if the instrument has the required properties (correlated with s_i but not with the original error term u_i), the OLS estimator in the second stage (being the IV estimator) is consistent. Essentially, the error term in the second stage is obtained by a transformation of the estimating equation, since $\beta\ \hat{s}_i$ is added to and subtracted from the original regression (1), yielding:

$$\varepsilon_i = u_i + \beta\ \left(s_i - \hat{s}_i\right)$$

This error term is uncorrelated with all the explanatory variables in the second stage regression ex_i, ex_i^2, and $\hat{s}_i$. This is why. Remember that $\hat{s}_i$ is just a linear combination of ex_i, ex_i^2, and f_i. The error term from the original equation (u_i) is by assumption uncorrelated with experience (and its square). And given the definition of an admissible instrumental variable, f_i should not be correlated (asymptotically) with the error term u_i. Thus there is no correlation between $\hat{s}_i$ and u_i. The term $s_i - \hat{s}_i$ is the residual from the first stage regression which was estimated by OLS and *by definition* is uncorrelated with the explanatory variables in that regression ex_i, ex_i^2, and f_i (see the Appendix to this chapter). Therefore there is no correlation between $\hat{s}_i$ and $s_i - \hat{s}_i$. Therefore in the second stage there is no correlation between the explanatory variables appearing in the equation (ex_i, ex_i^2, and $\hat{s}_i$) and the *transformed* error term (ε_i), and that is why a consistent estimate of β is obtained by applying OLS in the second stage.

In the following example, I have used data from the 2003 Labour Force Survey for France for individuals aged 25 to 54.[13] The data set contains father's and mother's occupation for nearly all respondents and these are converted into two dummy variables respectively, and take the value one when the parent is in an intermediate or high level occupation. The education variable is defined as the number of years of effective education obtained after the minimum school leaving age (that is validated by a diploma) and varies from zero to six. The other explanatory variables in the earnings equation are potential experience and its square, a dummy variable for females (fem_i), and a dummy variable for those living in the Paris region ($paris_i$). The dependent variable is the logarithm of hourly earnings. The model to be estimated is:

[13] In the CPS files I used above—the NBER Merged Outgoing Rotation Group—there were no reliable instrumental variables available.

$$\log w_i = \alpha + \beta\ s_i + \gamma_1 ex_i + \gamma_2 ex_i^2 + \delta_1\ fem_i + \delta_2\ paris_i + u_i$$

The parameter of interest is the return to an extra year of education. The ordinary least squares of β is 0.095 (see Table 1.3, column 1) which converts into a rate of return of 10% to an additional year of effective education. The coefficients on the experience variables are in line with those obtained for the United States above. Female workers are estimated to earn 12.2% less than males with identical characteristics, and persons living in the Paris region are estimated to receive 9.75% more than someone in Marseilles or elsewhere in France other things being equal. All the explanatory variables are significantly different from zero, and this set of variables can explain around a third of differences in log earnings.

It is possible that unobserved factors present in the error term are correlated with the education variable (ambition and drive, ability, and so forth) and if this is the case the OLS estimates will be biased. In order to examine whether such a correlation is present, a second set of estimates of the same parameters are obtained using the method of instrumental variables. Father's and mother's occupation are used as instruments. In order for this procedure to provide reliable estimates, the instruments must be correlated with the education variable. Using the two-stage least squares approach to IV estimation described above, the education variable is regressed on the two instrumental variables and on *all* the explanatory variables bar education. The results are present in the second column of Table 1.3. The education variable is strongly correlated with the two instruments—the t statistics are more than 4 times the critical value of 1.96. The F statistic for weak instruments proposed by Stock et al. (2002) of 141 confirms this strong correlation (the rule of thumb proposed was a statistic greater than 10).

Using these two instrumental variables for education in the earnings equation enables us to obtain an alternative set of estimates of the same parameters obtained using OLS (which appear in the first column of Table 1.3). If the IV estimates are different from the OLS estimates then we can conclude that the error term is correlated with the education variable. This is the hypothesis whose validity is examined by the Hausman test. The current case, adding the fitted value of education from the first stage regression to the original model, yields a coefficient of 0.04 (standard error of 0.015). The test statistic is 2.74 (5% critical value of 1.96) and so the hypothesis of zero correlation between the error term and the education variable is rejected. The IV method of estimation is therefore appropriate here and the results are presented in the third column of Table 1.3. The estimated value of β is 0.132 giving a rate of return of 14.1% ($\exp(0.132) - 1 = 0.141$), some

Table 1.3. OLS and IV estimates of the return to education in France

	Ordinary least squares	Two stage least squares	
		First stage regression	Instrumental variable estimates
Dependent	Log earnings	Education	Log earnings
Explanatory variable variables (mean in parentheses)	(mean = 2.18)		
Constant	1.56	−3.46	1.699
	(0.078)	(0.32)	(0.09)
Education (1.76)	0.095	–	0.133
	(0.003)		(0.015)
Experience (18.9)	0.038	0.141	0.032
	(0.008)	(0.03)	(0.008)
Experience squared (376)	−0.0006	0.006	−0.0009
	(0.0002)	(0.0008)	(0.0002)
Female (0.46)	−0.13	0.189	−0.141
	(0.007)	(0.03)	(0.008)
Paris area (0.15)	0.093	0.110	0.087
	(0.01)	(0.04)	(0.01)
Instrumental variables: Father skilled (0.16)	–	0.501	–
		(0.04)	
Mother skilled (0.07)	–	0.522	–
		(0.06)	
R^2	0.326	0.53	0.318
Number of observations	7251		
F statistic for two weak instruments	141.1		
Hausman test (1 additional regressor)		2.73 (5% critical value 1.96)	
Over-identification test (2 instruments, 1 degree of freedom)		3.34 (5% critical value 3.84)	

40% higher than the OLS estimate. This striking result indicates that there are unobserved factors correlated with the education level and this causes OLS to give biased estimates. In fact, OLS is found to underestimate the return to schooling—which is at odds with the suspicion that there is a positive correlation between unobserved factors and schooling.[14] The other parameters also change when estimated by IV but not to the same extent.

[14] This is a very common finding in empirical studies of earnings—see, for example, Angrist and Krueger (1991).

A final check on the adequacy of this approach is provided by the over-identification test that indicates that there is no correlation between one of the instruments and the equation error term. The test statistic is 3.34 which is below the 5% critical value of 3.84 from the chi squared distribution for one degree of freedom. Nothing can be said about the correlation with both instruments. The instrumental variables approach can be deemed as appropriate in this context on the basis of these three tests, and more confidence can be expressed in the IV estimates than the OLS estimates. The economically interesting question of why the IV estimate is higher than the OLS estimate is not answered.

This example shows how IV estimation is undertaken. The choice of instrumental variable is determined in part by its availability and in part by an ad hoc argument that children from well-to-do households have higher educational achievement and that, other than through this channel, coming from such a family environment does not improve earnings potential. This has to be the case since otherwise the chosen instrumental variables are not valid because they would be correlated with the error term. They must not be linked in any *direct* way to an individual's earnings. Other instrumental variables that have been used in practice include quarter of birth, changes in the age of compulsory schooling, existence of a further education college close to one's domicile, education subsidies, and parents' education. David Card (1999) provides a very thorough treatment of identifying and estimating the causal effect of education on earnings and these different instruments have been closely analysed in the literature on weak instruments.

1.4 Concluding Remarks

The use of linear models and OLS and instrumental variable estimation methods are the basic tools of applied econometric analysis. This is true of many sub-disciplines of economics and not just labour economics. The subsequent chapters build on the material presented here. In the next chapter more specific uses of these methods in labour economics and extensions to them are presented. In the present chapter it has been assumed that the sample used has been randomly drawn from, and is therefore representative of, a population of interest. In later chapters it will be seen that it is the limitations in the use of these tools that have given rise to alternative methods and approaches being developed, mainly due to the form of the data that are used. It is noteworthy that many of the techniques that have been developed have been so in order to deal with specific issues raised in a labour economics context.

Further Reading

For further details on applied regression analysis, thorough treatments are provided by Greene (2007) and Heij et al. (2004). The book by Berndt (1996) provides a very useful, practical approach and Goldberger (1991) spells out the statistical background to regression analysis in a particularly accessible manner. The graduate level texts on microeconometrics by Wooldridge (2002) and Cameron and Trivedi (2005) take the analysis further. An excellent applied treatment of earnings regression can be found in Blundell et al. (2005). While most texts contain a section on instrumental variables, Angrist and Pischke (2008) have a long chapter covering all the important issues in instrumental variables estimation and Angrist and Krueger (2001) provide an introductory perspective.

Appendix: The Mechanics of Ordinary Least Squares Estimation

Consider a simple two variable model with a constant term:

$$y_i = \beta_1 + x_{2i}\,\beta_2 + x_{3i}\,\beta_3 + u_i$$

The least squares rule determines estimates of the three parameters of this linear model ($\beta_1, \beta_2,$ and β_3) by creating a sum of squares and minimizing it with respect to these parameters. The term that is squared is the following deviation:

$$e_i = y_i - b_1 - x_{2i}\,b_2 - x_{3i}\,b_3$$

The sum of squares to be minimized is:

$$\begin{aligned} S &= e_1^2 + e_2^2 + \ldots + e_n^2 \\ &= \sum_{i=1}^{n} e_i^2 \end{aligned}$$

The partial derivatives are obtained with respect to $b_1,\ b_2,$ and b_3 as follows:

$$\frac{\partial S}{\partial b_1} = -2 \times \sum_{i=1}^{n} (y_i - b_1 - x_{2i}\,b_2 - x_{3i}\,b_3)$$

$$\frac{\partial S}{\partial b_2} = -2 \times \sum_{i=1}^{n} (y_i - b_1 - x_{2i}\,b_2 - x_{3i}\,b_3) \times x_{2i}$$

$$\frac{\partial S}{\partial b_3} = -2 \times \sum_{i=1}^{n} (y_i - b_1 - x_{2i}\,b_2 - x_{3i}\,b_3) \times x_{3i}.$$

Minimization requires that each of these derivatives be equal to zero. The values of $b_1,\ b_2,$ and b_3 that set these derivatives equal to zero are the OLS estimates of the population parameters, which we will call $\hat{\beta}_1,\ \hat{\beta}_2,$ and $\hat{\beta}_3$ respectively. These parameter estimates can be obtained by solving the following three equations:

$$\sum_{i=1}^{n} \left(y_i - \hat{\beta}_1 - x_{2i}\,\hat{\beta}_2 - x_{3i}\,\hat{\beta}_3\right) = 0$$

$$\sum_{i=1}^{n}\left(y_i - \hat{\beta}_1 - x_{2i}\,\hat{\beta}_2 - x_{3i}\,\hat{\beta}_3\right) \times x_{2i} = 0$$

and

$$\sum_{i=1}^{n}\left(y_i - \hat{\beta}_1 - x_{2i}\,\hat{\beta}_2 - x_{3i}\,\hat{\beta}_3\right) \times x_{3i} = 0$$

In practice this is achieved by writing the model in matrix form and the relevant formula is given in Section 1.1.2 of this chapter.

In each of the sums, the common term in brackets is called the *residual*:

$$\hat{u}_i = y_i - \hat{\beta}_1 - x_{2i}\,\hat{\beta}_2 - x_{3i}\,\hat{\beta}_3$$

Each sum can therefore be written in terms of the residual as follows:

$$\sum_{i=1}^{n}\hat{u}_i = 0 \quad \sum_{i=1}^{n}\hat{u}_i x_{2i} = 0 \quad \sum_{i=1}^{n}\hat{u}_i x_{3i} = 0$$

The *fitted value* of the dependent variable is $\hat{y}_i = \hat{\beta}_1 + x_{2i}\,\hat{\beta}_2 + x_{3i}\,\hat{\beta}_3$ and this is related to the *observed* value by the equality: $y_i = \hat{y}_i + \hat{u}_i$. Using this fact, the first of these three sums implies that

$$\frac{1}{n}\sum_{i=1}^{n} y_i = \frac{1}{n}\sum_{i=1}^{n}\hat{y}_i$$

or more succinctly: $\bar{y} = \bar{\hat{y}}$. The mean of the fitted values is equal to the mean of the dependent variable. In statistical jargon, the estimated conditional mean ($\bar{\hat{y}}$) is equal to the value of the unconditional mean ($\bar{y}$) in the sample. This property of least squares estimation is due to the presence of the constant term (β_1) in the model.

2

Further Regression Issues in Labour Economics

Estimating the parameters of interest of a model and checking that the model is a satisfactory representation of the relationship between the variables constitutes a first stage in applied econometrics. The results are interpreted in relation to underlying theoretical arguments and hypotheses of interest can be tested. In labour economics, the key aspects of the output of an econometric analysis are the marginal effects and the establishment of counterfactual situations. In this chapter, four aspects of regression analysis as used in labour economics are covered. Decomposing differences between groups—males and females, for example—is one of the key uses of econometric estimates, and this is treated in Section 2.1. The traditional way of undertaking a decomposition is to attribute part of the difference in the means of a variable (say earnings) for two groups to differences in characteristics, and the remainder to other factors. This is the Oaxaca decomposition of the difference in the means for two groups. Going beyond the average is made possible by using an approach that estimates the relationship between the dependent and explanatory variables at different points in the distribution. This is possible using quantile regression and is presented in the Section 2.2.

The econometric tools covered up to now apply essentially to cross-section data—data on a population at a given point in time. The increasing availability of panel data—in which the same individuals are followed over time—opens up interesting avenues for examining the empirical relationships in labour economics. In particular, individual specific effects can be identified and taken into account, thereby attenuating the effects of unobserved heterogeneity such as correlation between explanatory variables and the error term. Methods for analysing panel data are covered in Section 2.3. In the final part of this chapter, the issue of estimating standard errors is addressed. While this is often regarded as secondary to the estimation of the parameters of interest, it has become increasingly clear that applying a formula for estimating standard errors that is not applicable given the circumstances may give rise to false inferences and spurious relationships. This has led to the use of alternative approaches to calculating standard errors.

2.1 Decomposing Differences Between Groups—Oaxaca and Beyond

While the average private returns to different elements of human capital investment are of key interest, in a large number of studies earnings equations are used as a basis for comparing the earnings outcomes for different groups of employees, such as males and females. A lower return to human capital for female employees could be evidence of labour market discrimination against women, while lower earnings due to women having on average fewer years of labour market experience is not. In order to assess the relative importance of these different sources of earnings differences, Oaxaca (1973) has proposed[1] a widely used decomposition of the gap between the mean of log earnings for the two groups. This involves first estimating the earnings equation separately for the two groups:

$$y_i^M = \sum_{k=1}^{K} x_{ki}^M \beta_k^M + u_i^M \quad y_i^F = \sum_{k=1}^{K} x_{ki}^F \beta_k^F + u_i^F \tag{2.1}$$

The Oaxaca decomposition uses the fact that if the parameter vector includes a constant then the average value of the OLS residual in each equation is zero (see the Appendix to Chapter 1) and so, for the estimated parameters, the following equalities hold:

$$\bar{y}^M = \bar{x}^{M'} \hat{\beta}^M \quad \text{and} \quad \bar{y}^F = \bar{x}^{F'} \hat{\beta}^F$$

where $\bar{x}^{j'} \hat{\beta}^j = \sum_{k=1}^{K} \bar{x}_k^j \hat{\beta}_k^j$ and $j = F, M$ The difference between the means of log earnings is:

$$\bar{y}^M - \bar{y}^F = \bar{x}^{M'} \hat{\beta}^M - \bar{x}^{F'} \hat{\beta}^F$$

By adding and subtracting $\bar{x}^{F'} \hat{\beta}^M$ on the right-hand side, the difference can then be expressed as

[1] A similar approach was put forward by Blinder (1973).

$$\bar{y}^M - \bar{y}^F = \left(\bar{x}^M - \bar{x}^F\right)' \hat{\beta}^M + \bar{x}^{F'} \left(\hat{\beta}^M - \hat{\beta}^F\right)$$

$$\Delta = E + U \tag{2.2}$$

This is referred to as the *aggregate* decomposition. Sometimes each of the components is expressed as a proportion of the overall difference. The first component, E, measures the part of the difference in means, Δ, which is due to differences in the average characteristics of the two groups; the second, U, is due to differences in the estimated coefficients. The latter can also be interpreted as the 'unexplained' part of the difference in means of y and be attributable to discrimination. The reasoning is as follows. In order to compare what is comparable, if female employees had the same average characteristics as the average male $\bar{x}^F = \bar{x}^M$, the first term of the decomposition disappears ($E = 0$) leaving a difference in earnings which is due solely to differential returns to human capital investments.

This is illustrated in Fig. 2.1 for a single variable, in a bivariate regression with a constant term:

$$y_i = \alpha_0 + \alpha_1 z_i + v_i$$

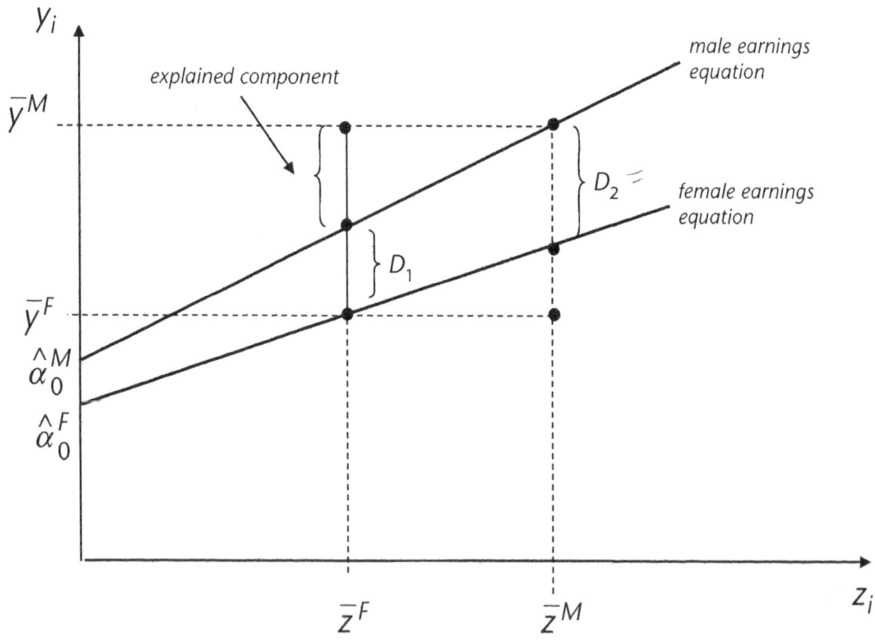

Figure 2.1. The Oaxaca decomposition

Table 2.1. Oaxaca decomposition of gender earnings differences in the United Kingdom

Log earnings	Means		Overall difference	Characteristics effect		Unexplained difference*
	Males	Females				
	2.477	2.246	0.231	−0.0046		0.236
	$\bar{x}_k^M$	$\bar{x}_k^F$	$\hat{\beta}_k^M$	$\left(\bar{x}_k^{M'} - \bar{x}_k^{F'}\right)\hat{\beta}_k^M$	$\hat{\beta}_k^F$	$\bar{x}_k^{F'}\left(\hat{\beta}_k^M - \hat{\beta}_k^F\right)$
Constant	1	1	1.711 (0.03)	0	1.596 (0.026)	0.115
Education	3.867	3.923	0.0875 (0.004)	−0.0049	0.0982 (0.003)	−0.042
Experience	22.36	21.916	0.0407 (0.0025)	0.018	0.0225 (0.002)	0.397
Experience squared	647.13	623.187	−0.00074 (0.00005)	−0.018	−0.00037 (0.00005)	−0.234
R^2			0.26		0.27	

Chow test F (4, 5802) = 123.1 (p = 0.000)
Standard errors are in parentheses
*The sum is not exact due to rounding

Because the average values of log earnings (y) and of characteristic z_i are higher for males, part of the log earnings difference is explained by the difference in $\bar{z}$. The remaining, unexplained part is the difference between what the average female would have earned if she had been paid on the same basis as an equivalent male worker and what she actually earns. This is given by the distance D_1, which is referred to as the discrimination component of the Oaxaca decomposition and can be viewed as a *residual* in that it is the part of the mean difference that is unexplained by differences in characteristics.

An alternative way of measuring discrimination is to calculate what a male with average characteristics would have earned if he were treated in the same way as a typical female worker, and compare that with what he actually earns. This time the discrimination component is given by the distance D_2. In general, the two measures diverge ($D_1 \neq D_2$)—they are identical only when the slope parameters (α_1) are the same for both groups of workers. This is called the *index number problem.*[2]

Table 2.1 presents the results of an Oaxaca decomposition for the United Kingdom in 2007. The data are taken from the British Household Panel Survey, for individuals declaring both earnings and hours of work for the pay period prior to interview. Education is measured as years of education after the minimum school leaving age, and potential rather than actual

[2] The index number problem exists because the decomposition of the same difference in means could equally be obtained by adding and subtracting $\bar{x}^{M'}\hat{\beta}^F$ in which case it is expressed as $\left(\bar{x}^M - \bar{x}^F\right)'\hat{\beta}^F + \bar{x}^{M'}\left(\hat{\beta}^M - \hat{\beta}^F\right)$.

experience is used. The basic Mincer earnings equation is estimated separately for males and females. The difference in the means of log earnings is 0.231, representing a raw wage gap of 26%. Since females have more education on average (3.92 years compared to 3.87), and differences in experience are cancelled out by the concave relationship between log earnings and experience, the explained part of the difference is negative: in other words, if females had the same returns to education and experience as males, they would earn more than males on average. However, the coefficients of the two equations are not the same and apart from the return to education, the coefficients are higher for males. Thus the different elements of the unexplained component are the key determinants of earnings differences between males and females in the United Kingdom. The difference between the two constant terms alone accounts for half of the raw wage gap.

The decomposition is widely used in order to distinguish group differences in earnings due to endowments or characteristics on the one hand and the pecuniary return to those characteristics on the other. Since the latter is simply a difference between two groups of coefficients, it is natural to examine whether the difference in returns between the two groups is significant. A statistical test of the presence of discrimination is therefore a test of the null hypothesis $H_0 : \{ \beta_1^M = \beta_1^F, \beta_2^M = \beta_2^F, ..., \beta_K^M = \beta_K^F \}$ in equation (2.1)—which is just a Chow test. In the case of the example above, the Chow test of the equality of the four coefficients in the earnings equation categorically rejects the null hypothesis (see Table 2.1). The Chow test is used for all coefficients taken together. However, it is possible to identify those factors that are the main reasons for differences in returns. This involves calculating the effect of each variable taken on its own, and testing to see whether there is a statistically significant difference in the return to that variable between the two groups.

An approach which is equivalent to estimating separate equations for the two groups is obtained if the two groups are pooled into a single sample, with the constant term and each explanatory variable interacted with a dummy variable which takes the value $d_i = 1$ for females and $d_i = 0$ for males. The equation to be estimated for the pooled sample is then:

$$y_i = \sum_{k=1}^{K} x_{ki}\beta_k + \sum_{k=1}^{K} (d_i x_{ki})\ \delta_k + u_i \tag{2.3}$$

A typical coefficient for males will be $\beta_k^M = \beta_k$, and for females $\beta_k^F = \beta_k + \delta_k$. OLS estimates of these parameters will be identical to those obtained above when separate equations were used for males and females. The coefficients in the second sum, the $\delta_k = \beta_k^F - \beta_k^M$, indicate whether or not there is discrimination—that is, whether the return on characteristics for females is different compared to males. The hypothesis $H_0^* : \delta_k = 0$ is equivalent to $H_0 : \beta_k^M = \beta_k^F$, so that a simple t test can be used to establish the principal sources of discrimination. If the hypothesis $H_0^* : \delta_k = 0$ is not rejected for a given variable (x_{ik}), then the return to that variable is not a source of earnings discrimination.

The contribution of each variable to the explained part can be measured as:

$$c_k = \left(\bar{x}_k^M - \bar{x}_k^F\right)\hat{\beta}_k^M \quad \text{for} \quad k = 2,\ 3, \ldots., K$$

and this is sometimes expressed in terms of a proportion of the explained differential:

$$c_k^* = \frac{c_k}{\left(\bar{x}^M - \bar{x}^F\right)'\hat{\beta}^M} \quad \text{and} \quad \sum_{k=2}^{K} c_k^* = 1$$

This is referred to as the *detailed decomposition*, as opposed to the aggregate decomposition in equation (2.2).

The Oaxaca decomposition is a useful tool but it must be applied carefully. Changing the equation specification will alter the size of the unexplained part or residual. This is a germane question since factors other than human capital variables influence earnings. Variables such as regional dummies, measures of health status, and periods of unemployment in the past could all be justifiably included in an earnings regression. More debatable is the inclusion of occupational and sectoral dummies, since there may be crowding of females into particular jobs. Furthermore, in the same way as the index number issue, there is also a question of identification when some of the explanatory variables are dummies as, for example, when education in terms of diploma obtained, rather than the number of years of education. While the aggregate decomposition is unchanged, the choice of reference category alters the constant and the contribution of the individual variables in a detailed decomposition.

By pooling males and females into one sample, a number of useful extensions of the Oaxaca decomposition are possible. In the standard decomposition, the discrimination component is the net effect of two underlying mechanisms: (i) paying one group a lower wage and (ii) paying the preferred group a premium. Oaxaca and Ransom (1994) refer to these as the *pure discrimination* and *nepotism* components, respectively, based on the theory of discrimination put forward by Becker (1973). A first extension uses the OLS estimates of $\beta_k^M = \beta_k$, $\beta_k^F = \beta_k + \delta_k$ and the estimates of β_k^* obtained from the following pooled regression:

$$y_i = \sum_{k=1}^{K} x_{ki}\beta_k^* + u_i$$

The underlying argument in this framework is that β_k^* is an estimate of the non-discriminatory return to characteristic, x_k. By adding and subtracting each of the following terms, $\bar{x}^{M'}\hat{\beta}^*$ and $\bar{x}^{F'}\hat{\beta}^*$, the mean difference can be decomposed using OLS estimates $\hat{\beta}^*$, $\hat{\beta}^M$, and $\hat{\beta}^F$ as:

$$\bar{y}^M - \bar{y}^F = \bar{x}^{M'}\hat{\beta}^M - \bar{x}^{F'}\hat{\beta}^F + \bar{x}^{M'}\hat{\beta}^* - \bar{x}^{M'}\hat{\beta}^* + \bar{x}^{F'}\hat{\beta}^* - \bar{x}^{F'}\hat{\beta}^*$$

$$= \left(\bar{x}^{M'} - \bar{x}^F\right)'\hat{\beta}^* + \bar{x}^{M'}\left(\hat{\beta}^M - \hat{\beta}^*\right) + \bar{x}^{F'}\left(\hat{\beta}^* - \hat{\beta}^F\right)$$

The first component is the part of the difference that is justified by differences in characteristics, the second term measures nepotism—employers favour male employees—while the third component represents the earnings loss for females due to discrimination, that is what the average female would have earned in the absence of discrimination *and* nepotism compared to what she actually earns. In the example for the United Kingdom, Table 2.2 presents the pooled estimates and the three components. Nepotism is estimated to account for most of the raw gender earnings gap (53%), while the discrimination component represents 48%, and differences in characteristics, −1%.

In order for Oaxaca decompositions to be exact, each earnings equation has to contain a constant term (so that $x_{1i} = 1$). In equation (2.3), the common constant term β_1 will be obtained in the first sum in the equation, and the constant term for females will be $\beta_1 + \delta_1$. The presence of the common constant term will mean that the estimated OLS residual from this equation, $\hat{u}_i$, will have a mean equal to zero. However, for each of the two gender groups, the mean estimated residual will be different and

Table 2.2. Oaxaca–Ransom decomposition of gender earnings differences in the United Kingdom

Overall difference: 0.231		Characteristic's effect	Nepotism*	Discrimination*
	Pooled Estimates	−0.0045	0.1244	0.1117
	$\hat{\beta}_k^*$	$\left(\bar{x}_k^{M'} - \bar{x}_k^{F'}\right)\hat{\beta}_k^*$	$\bar{x}_k^{M'}\left(\hat{\beta}_k^M - \hat{\beta}_k^*\right)$	$\bar{x}_k^{F'}\left(\hat{\beta}_k^* - \hat{\beta}_k^F\right)$
Constant	1.65 (0.021)		0.0606	0.0543
Education	0.0927 (0.0026)	−0.0052	−0.0201	−0.0217
Experience	0.0315 (0.0017)	0.014	0.2057	0.1957
Experience squared	−0.00056 (0.00004)	−0.0133	−0.122	−0.1177
R^2	0.243			

Standard errors are in parentheses

*The sum is not exact due to rounding

the distributions of the estimated residual can be compared. Juhn, Murphy, and Pierce (1993) have proposed a decomposition which seeks to take into account the distribution of the residual, which they interpret as unobserved productivity differences.

Juhn, Murphy, and Pierce (1993) make the assumption that the male equation represents earnings determination in the absence of discrimination, and that the parameters of the male earnings equation when estimated by OLS are unbiased. The counter-factual earnings level for a female worker with given characteristics can be calculated using the male parameter estimates and the unexplained part can be obtained using the estimated male residual. This is done by ordering the female sample by the value of the residual and determining for each female member of this sample a residual corresponding to the residual at the same quantile of the male distribution. A female at 10% from the bottom of her distribution will be allocated the residual for a male who is 10% from the bottom of his distribution. Call this rank-determined residual $\tilde{u}_{Fi}$, so that $\tilde{u}_{Fi} > 0$ for a female with favourable unobserved characteristics. In the Juhn, Murphy, and Pierce (JMP) framework, the counter-factual earnings of a female with characteristics x_{Fi} are given by:

$$y_i^F = \sum_{k=1}^{K} x_{ki}^F \hat{\beta}_k^M + \hat{\sigma}^M \left(\frac{\tilde{u}_i^F}{\hat{\sigma}^M} \right)$$

where $\hat{\beta}^M$ and $\hat{\sigma}^M$ are the OLS estimates of the parameter vector and equation standard error, respectively. If we call $\theta_i^j = \frac{\tilde{u}_i^j}{\hat{\sigma}^M}$ (for males $\tilde{u}_{Mi} = \hat{u}_{Mi}$) the standardized residual, the equivalent of the Oaxaca decomposition is:

$$\bar{y}^M - \bar{y}^F = \left(\bar{x}^M - \bar{x}^F\right)' \hat{\beta}^M + \hat{\sigma}^M \left[\bar{\theta}^M - \bar{\theta}^F\right]$$

The second term is by definition numerically identical to the term $\bar{x}^{F'} \left(\hat{\beta}^M - \hat{\beta}^F\right)$ in the Oaxaca approach and, although it appears in the decomposition, in fact the mean of the estimated male residual is zero and so $\bar{\theta}^M = 0$. Thus in the JMP set-up, the discrimination component is explicitly treated as the unexplained or *residual* part of the difference in average (log) earnings. Furthermore, only the estimates of the male earnings equation are required for this decomposition.

In practice, the standard application of the JMP decomposition is the examination of changes in the earnings difference over time. Defining the change in mean of y for males between period 0 and period 1 as $\Delta\bar{y}^M = \bar{y}_1^M - \bar{y}_0^M$ and the change in the earnings gap as $\Delta = \Delta\bar{y}^M - \Delta\bar{y}^F$, the JMP decomposition is as follows:

$$\Delta = \left(\Delta\bar{x}^M - \Delta\bar{x}^F\right) \hat{\beta}_0^M + \left(\bar{x}^M - \bar{x}^F\right)' \left(\hat{\beta}_1^M - \hat{\beta}_0^M\right) + \left(\hat{\sigma}_1^M - \hat{\sigma}_0^M\right) \left(\bar{\theta}^M - \bar{\theta}^F\right) +$$
$$\hat{\sigma}_0^M \left(\Delta\bar{\theta}^M - \Delta\bar{\theta}^F\right)$$

This enables the time change in the gender gap to be divided into the four components on the right-hand side, which are changes related to changes (i) in average characteristics, (ii) in returns to those characteristics, (iii) in returns to unobservables, and (iv) to changes in unobservables, respectively.

As in many areas of the econometric analysis of labour market phenomena, ongoing research is aimed at improving upon existing methods and the same is true for decomposing differences between groups. Currently attention is concentrated on looking at differences in the *distributions* of earnings (and other variables) between groups. Recent work has generalized the Oaxaca approach to take into account higher moments of the distribution of earnings when comparing groups (see, for example, Dinardo, Fortin, and Lemieux, 1996, and Donald, Green, and Paarsch, 2002)—often referred to as 'going beyond the mean'. These and other decomposition methods are treated very comprehensively by Firpo, Fortin, and Lemieux (2010). One such method is based on the quantile regression approach, to which we now turn.

2.2 Quantile Regression and Earnings Decompositions

As pointed out in Chapter 1, a linear regression picks out the average relationship between the dependent and explanatory variables. However, in a context where there is substantial heterogeneity, there is a strong case for examining other dimensions of a relationship than the mean. Furthermore, the mean is sensitive to outliers and this may have an effect on parameter estimates and, in many studies, researchers simply omit such observations. In both of these situations quantile regression is a useful tool. While Koenker and Bassett (1978) introduced quantile regression in the 1970s, it is only recently that it has been used as a standard tool; that is, since estimation has been rendered straightforward by computing technology.

A useful of way of envisaging quantile regression is as follows. Whereas ordinary least squares regression estimates the conditional expectation $E(y_i|x_i) = x_i'\beta$, a quantile regression estimates the θth conditional quantile:

$$Q_\theta(y_i|x_i) = x_i'\beta_\theta$$

so that the conditional median relationship is estimated when $\theta = 0.5$—the quantile regression estimator for the median is also referred to as the least absolute deviations estimator. It is important to recognize that what is modelled is the θth quantile of y for a given value of x—it is a conditional quantile.

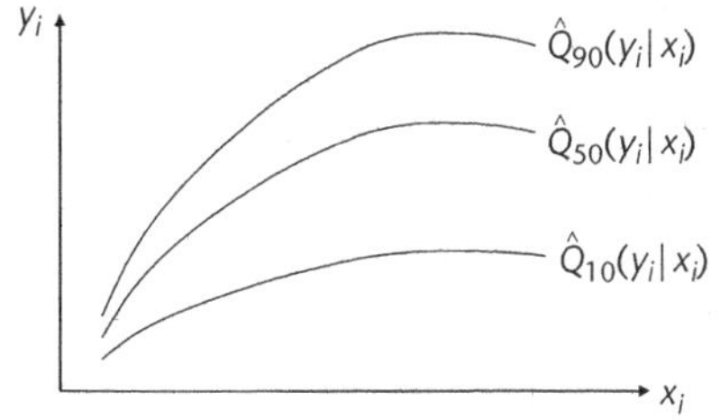

Figure 2.2. Conditional quantiles

Quantile regression enables the impact of changes in explanatory variables on the dependent variable to differ at different points in the (conditional) distribution instead of concentrating solely on the effect on the average as in linear regression. Indeed, if the actual relationship between the variables is linear with a symmetrically distributed error term, the regression lines for each quantile are parallel and vary only by a constant. Quantile regression becomes interesting when there is heteroscedasticity or non-constant parameters (see Fig. 2.2). For example, it is possible that in low wage labour markets, returns to education and experience are lower. Estimating the Mincer earnings equation for the US data used in Chapter 1 using quantile regression suggests this is so (see Table 2.3).

The return to education is quite different in the tails of the distribution while the median return is similar to the OLS estimate. Returns to experience are also higher further up the conditional earnings distribution. After 10 years experience, the lowest quintile return to a further year is 1.8%, while the median and highest quintile returns are 2.9% and 3.6% respectively. Returns become negative after around 28 years of experience whatever the quantile.

In contrast to the OLS estimator, there is no explicit formula for the quantile regression estimator, and so arguments about bias, efficiency, and consistency are not straightforward to present. Research into the statistical properties of quantile regression is ongoing and Koenker (2005) provides a very thorough treatment of the current state of knowledge.

Table 2.3. Quantile regression estimates of the US earnings equation

	OLS estimates	$\theta = 0.2$	$\theta = 0.5$	$\theta = 0.8$
Constant	0.947	1.003	0.835	0.867
Education	0.074	0.053	0.079	0.094
Experience	0.041	0.028	0.045	0.056
Experience squared	−0.00075	−0.0005	−0.0008	−0.001

As with linear regression, it is possible to undertake decompositions with quantile regression. It is more complicated, however, since the passage between the unconditional difference in earnings at a given quantile is not equal to the conditional difference. Recall that the difference in unconditional means $(\bar{y}^M - \bar{y}^F)$ on the left-hand side is equal to the difference between the estimated OLS conditional means $(\bar{x}^{M'}\hat{\beta}^M - \bar{x}^{F'}\hat{\beta}^F)$ on the right-hand side (when there is a constant term in the regression). This equivalence does not exist for quantile regression—see Firpo, Fortin, and Lemieux (2010) for the technical details. This makes the decomposition more complicated to perform since the conditional quantiles have to be linked to the unconditional differences and this requires simulation methods.

Mata and Machado (2005) propose a method based on the counterfactual interpretation of the Oaxaca decomposition. In order to create the explained and unexplained components, the Oaxaca approach introduces the counterfactual term $(\bar{x}^{F'}\hat{\beta}^M)$, which measures what an average female would have earned had she been male. Mata and Machado calculate the counter-factual wage for each quantile using simulations to calculate the quantiles of the counter-factual distribution.

2.3 Regression with Panel Data

The tools described thus far are appropriate when cross-section data are used so that the sample is drawn from a population at a given point in time. If the same individuals are observed at several points in time (each year, say) then the influence of any unobserved variable that does not change over time can be determined and/or modelled. A classic example is unobserved intellectual ability, which will not vary over time (or at least not over the horizon relevant for earnings determination), and ability will clearly be correlated with years of education. Data sets which contain a cross-section of individuals (or households, firms, geographical areas) each of whom is followed over a period of time are called *panel data* sets (and sometimes longitudinal data). Apart from providing a larger sample, panel data also enable individual specific effects to be introduced into a model. To see this, we rewrite the basic linear model with a double subscript—i represents an individual and t a year:

$$y_{it} = x'_{it}\beta + u_{it} \quad i = 1, 2, \ldots n \quad t = 1, 2, \ldots T$$

Note firstly that the sample size has increased by a factor of $T \geq 2$ and so even if the longitudinal nature of the data is ignored, the use of panel data provides more accurate estimates of the parameters of interest. The OLS estimator of β in this equation is referred to as the *pooled estimator*. If there is individual-specific unobserved heterogeneity, this will be present in the error term and represented by α_i:

$$u_{it} = \alpha_i + \varepsilon_{it} \quad \text{where} \quad \varepsilon_{it} \sim iid\left(0\,,\,\sigma_\varepsilon^2\right)$$

The error term ε_{it} is the usual error term picking up non systematic factors that influence y_{it}. Since α_i does not vary over time it can be either estimated or modelled, that is its influence is taken into account. If α_j is considered as a 'fixed effect'—specific to individual sample member j and time-invariant—it can be estimated by defining a dummy variable $D^j_{jt} = 1$, $D^j_{it} = 0 \;\; i \neq j$ for each individual and including it in the estimating model:

$$y_{it} = \sum_{j=1}^{n} \alpha_j D^j_{it} + x'_{it}\beta + \varepsilon_{it} \tag{2.4}$$

For any given individual, only one of the dummies will be equal to one, and so the equation becomes:

$$y_{it} = \alpha_i + x'_{it}\beta + \varepsilon_{it}$$

This specification purges the OLS estimator of the vector β of any bias emanating from a correlation between time-invariant unobserved heterogeneity and the explanatory variables x_{it}. In short, because α_i and x_{it} are both in the model, any correlation between them cannot affect the error term ε_{it}. The OLS estimator of the vector β in this model is usually called the *least squares dummy variable* (LSDV) estimator.

The downside of this approach is that it involves estimating as many fixed effect parameters α_i as there are individuals in the panel. The total number of parameters to be estimated will be $n + K$. However, estimating all these parameters simultaneously can be avoided by transforming the equation in order to eliminate the $\sum_{j=1}^{n} \alpha_j D^j_{it}$ term.[3] This involves subtracting the mean for each individual ($\bar{y}_i$ and $\bar{x}_i$) from the y_{it} and x_{it} variables, respectively, and estimating parameters of the model:

$$y_{it} - \bar{y}_i = (x_{it} - \bar{x}_i)'\,\beta + v_{it} \tag{2.5}$$

In this equation there are only the K parameters in the vector β to be estimated. The OLS estimator of β in the transformed equation is referred to as the *within* estimator. The fixed effects—if required—can be estimated indirectly by $\hat{\alpha}_i = \bar{y}_i - \bar{x}'_i\hat{\beta}$.

[3] This amounts to applying the Frisch–Waugh–Lovell theorem, see Davidson and MacKinnon (1993).

A number of points are worth noting here. First, while the dimension of the problem has been diminished (from $n+K$ to a mere K parameters), the 'within' transformation that converts the explanatory variables from x_{it} to $x_{it}-\bar{x}_i$, means that the coefficient of any explanatory variable that does not vary over time cannot be identified since $x_{kit}=\bar{x}_{ki}$ for all periods, so that $x_{kit}-\bar{x}_{ki}=0$. In the context of the Mincer equation, in a fixed effects framework it is not possible to identify the return to education since, for the vast majority, years of education do not change once an individual has entered the labour market. The same is true with the dummy variable specification. The effect of unchanging variables such as gender and race cannot be identified either. Second, the fixed effect is 'in the model' and not in the error term, and thus any time-invariant unobserved heterogeneity is removed. Any correlation between the error term and the explanatory variables is thus removed, and so the within estimator is unbiased. It applies when the individual-specific component α_i is treated as a fixed effect specific to each sample member. It is the variation of the x_{it} around the mean for each individual $\bar{x}_i$—the 'within variation'—that provides the variation needed to identify the parameters of the model. Third, the within estimator is numerically identical to the value of the vector β obtained in the specification containing dummy variables.[4] The standard errors need to be estimated using the within transformed explanatory variables. Fourth, panel data mean that there is a time or temporal dimension to the observations. The periods $t=1$ and $t>1$ may not be fully comparable (one could think of earnings during an upswing and during a recession). Practitioners often include a dummy variable for each of the periods covered—'time dummies'—in the analysis (bar one in order to avoid the 'dummy variable trap'). These are defined as follows: $T^s_{is}=1$ if $t=s$ and $T^s_{it}=0$ if $t\neq s$ and the model is now:

$$y_{it}=\sum_{j=1}^{n}\alpha_j D^j_{it}+\sum_{s=2}^{T}\gamma_s T^s_{it}+x'_{it}\beta+\varepsilon_{it}$$

For a given individual (only one individual dummy is equal to one) in a given period (only one time dummy is equal to one), the equation is:

$$y_{it}=\alpha_i+x'_{it}\beta+\gamma_t+\varepsilon_{it}$$

The coefficients on the time dummies pick up any shocks, events, and changes of economic environment that are common to all members of the panel, and their impact on the dependent variable is given by γ_t in period t. Fifth, and also due to the time dimension, it is possible that the error term purged of the fixed effect is correlated over time. This could occur if there is

[4] This is precisely what the Frisch–Waugh–Lovell theorem states and why it is useful.

time-varying unobserved individual heterogeneity. Finally, the fixed effects estimator of individual effect, α_i, is unbiased but not consistent—essentially the variance of the OLS estimator does not converge asymptotically to zero (the second condition for consistency in Tchebyschev's lemma—see Chapter 1). This is because, by treating the individual-specific component as a fixed effect, the estimated effect is specific to the member of a sample and does not generalize to an individual chosen at random from the population. This is why modelling the distribution of the individual effects can be more efficient.

The inability of the fixed effects estimator (LSDV or within) to identify certain parameters of interest is an important disadvantage in many labour economics applications. An alternative approach is to treat the individual-specific effect not as a fixed effect for each sample member, but rather as a value taken from a distribution such as $\alpha_i \sim N\left(\alpha,\ \sigma_\alpha^2\right)$. This means that the individual effect is not specific to the sample as in the case of fixed effects but is a random variable. Instead of estimating its value, the alternative approach is to model its distribution.

The econometric model is as before except that the individual effect is now an unobserved component that is incorporated into the error term:

$$y_{it} = \alpha + x_{it}'\beta + u_{it} \quad i = 1, 2, \ldots n \quad t = 1, 2, \ldots T$$
$$u_{it} = (\alpha_i - \alpha) + \varepsilon_{it} \quad \text{where} \quad \varepsilon_{it} \sim iid\left(0\ ,\ \sigma_\varepsilon^2\right)$$

In order for the error term to have a zero mean, the mean of the distribution of α_i becomes the constant in the model. After this modification, the error term in the model u_{it} will have the following properties:

$$E\left(u_{it}\right) = 0 \quad \text{var}\left(u_{it}\right) = \sigma_\alpha^2 + \sigma_\varepsilon^2 \quad \text{cov}\left(u_{it}, u_{is}\right) = \sigma_\alpha^2$$

The non-zero covariance (a bit like serial correlation in time series specifications) means that OLS estimation, while sufficient for unbiased estimation of the parameters α and β, is not the most efficient. Generalized least squares and maximum likelihood estimation use more information and have in theory smaller variances for the parameter estimates. Most importantly in the current context is that it is possible to obtain estimates of all the parameters of interest including those pertaining to time invariant explanatory variables such as education and gender. The resulting estimator is called the *random effects estimator* (as opposed to the fixed effects estimators (LSDV and within)). This estimator involves obtaining estimates of σ_α^2 and σ_ε^2 (from preliminary OLS regressions) and then transforming the model in a similar way to the within estimator as:

$$y_{it} - \theta\,\bar{y}_i = \alpha + (x_{it} - \theta\,\bar{x}_i)'\,\beta + u_{it}^G \quad \text{where} \quad \theta = 1 - \sqrt{\frac{\sigma_\varepsilon^2}{\sigma_\varepsilon^2 + T\sigma_\alpha^2}}$$

Unlike the within estimator though, the random effects approach uses information on the variation of variables between the observations and not simply the 'within' individual dimension. For this reason it is in theory more efficient. There is however a downside since, as stated at the outset, one of the advantages of panel data was precisely to be able to eliminate the bias created by correlation between (time invariant) unobserved heterogeneity and the explanatory variables. The random effects estimator will be biased if there is such a correlation since it creates a correlation between the equation error and the explanatory variables:

$$corr\,(x_{it},\ u_{it}) = corr\,(x_{it},\ \alpha_i + \varepsilon_{it}) = corr\,(x_{it},\ \alpha_i) \neq 0$$

Therefore it is preferable to use a fixed effects estimator as a general rule. The fixed effects estimator does not identify all of the parameters of interest but is generally unbiased and the random effects estimator is most likely to be biased. It is possible to use a Hausman-type test to distinguish between the fixed effects and random effects estimators for time varying explanatory variables *only*, but because of the limited scope of this test, it may be of little practical value in many labour economics applications.

2.4 Estimating Standard Errors

In the first chapter it was pointed out that two methods of estimating the standard errors of parameter estimates are generally used according to whether heteroscedasticity is thought to be present or not. In this final section we look at some alternative ways of estimating standard errors that are being increasingly used in practice. This is partly due to concern that not all the information available is being used, and partly because the formulae used for estimating standard errors (both OLS and White) may not be accurate. For example, it was pointed out earlier that most practitioners simply present heteroscedasticity-consistent standard errors (HCSE) as derived by White (1980). Being consistent, these are reliable in large samples when there is heteroscedasticity. However, when there is little or no heteroscedasticity it turns out that these estimates are biased downwards and, what is more, they can be more biased than the OLS estimated standard errors. These problems can be attenuated by correcting the formula for calculating the HCSEs (see Davidson and MacKinnon, 1993, for a thorough discussion and suggestions of ways of correcting these deficiencies).

One of the key issues is that the formulae used for calculating the standard errors of estimated coefficients are only valid in certain conditions. For example, the formula for OLS standard errors is based on unbiased estimation of the parameters and the error term being independently and identically distributed (*iid*). When determined according to a formula in this way, or using White's 'sandwich' equation, the standard errors are said to be *analytically* determined. Alternative approaches, made easily accessible by advances in computer technology, use simulation methods. One of the more appealing is the *bootstrap method* since it determines the standard errors not by inventing data but by re-sampling the same data used to obtain the parameter estimates. Here is a brief description of how it works in the case where the sample is drawn at random from a population.

If the sample contains 1,000 observations, a bootstrap sample is obtained by picking one of the observations at random, saving its value (in a data file), and putting it back into the original sample. This called sampling *with replacement*. A second observation is then selected at random, saved in the data file and the observation put back into the pot. This is repeated 1,000 times so that there are 1,000 randomly selected observations in the data file (the same number as in the original sample). Some observations from the original sample will be selected several times while others are not selected at all. Using this generated sample, the parameters of the model are estimated using the relevant technique. These estimated parameters are saved (in an output file). Another sample is generated in the same manner and another set of parameter estimates are obtained and saved. This process is repeated say 5,000 times, and so there are 5,000 estimates of each parameter. Using these, the standard error of a parameter can be calculated by applying the formula used in descriptive statistics. So for parameter β_k the bootstrap standard error is calculated as:

$$\text{b.se}\left(\hat{\beta}_{km}\right) = \sqrt{\frac{1}{4999}\sum_{m=1}^{5000}\left(\hat{\beta}_{km} - \overline{\hat{\beta}}_k\right)^2}$$

Alternatively, the 2.5% and 97.5% quantiles of the distribution of the $\hat{\beta}_k$ can be used to construct a 95% confidence interval. The bootstrap technique has the advantage of not depending on an analytical formula that is valid only in the circumstances used for its derivation. For example, if the sample size is limited, one may have little confidence in applying a formula that is valid only when the sample size tends to infinity. In a linear regression with or without heteroscedasticity, so long as the sample is chosen at random there is no real need to use the bootstrap.

A final issue raised here is when variables for units of different dimensions are used in the same equation, such as the effect of the local unemployment rate on individual earnings. The concern for the standard errors arises because several individuals may come from the same local area. This could give rise to an 'intra-class' correlation between the error terms in the equation for the individuals in that area. This is in fact reminiscent of the error correlation encountered in the random effects model and examined in the previous section. One way of examining this is to assume that the error term contains two components. The model for individual i who belongs to class c is written as:

$$y_{ic} = \alpha + x'_{ic}\beta + u_{ic} \quad \text{where} \quad u_{ic} = \alpha_c + \varepsilon_{ic}$$

Using the results established for the random effects model above, the error term u_{ic} is not independent across observations on individuals (i and j) in the same class c since:

$$\text{cov}\left(u_{ic}, u_{jc}\right) = \sigma_\alpha^2 \quad \text{and} \quad \rho = \frac{\text{cov}\left(u_{ic}, u_{jc}\right)}{\sqrt{\text{var}\left(u_{ic}\right)\text{var}\left(u_{jc}\right)}} = \frac{\sigma_\alpha^2}{\sigma_\alpha^2 + \sigma_\varepsilon^2}$$

The intra-class correlation measured by ρ is the important factor here, since if $\rho = 0$ there no problem. However, even if ρ is small (say 0.05) the OLS estimated standard errors can be strongly biased downwards, giving the impression that coefficients are very significant when in fact they are not. This bias was illustrated in a labour economics context by Moulton (1990) using state level variables in a Mincer-type earnings equation. He included state level variables that are irrelevant for earnings, such as total land area and the height of the highest hill or mountain in metres. On the basis of the OLS standard errors, both variables are found to have a statistically significant impact on individual earnings. He estimates ρ to be 0.03 and when he uses an analytically correct formula for the standard errors, none of the state-level variables are found to be significant. This is reminiscent of 'spurious regression'—where the standard test procedures indicate the presence of a relation between the variables when in fact none exists—which is often encountered when using non-stationary time series data.

The various methods of estimating standard errors are usually available in econometric software. In certain estimation procedures, the appropriate standard errors are presented automatically. As has been suggested on several occasions here, it is probably a good idea when in doubt to see whether the results change when passing from one method to another. If a coefficient is significantly different from zero whichever method is used to estimate the standard errors, then there is reason to have confidence that this conclusion is sound. However, if it is significant with one set of standard errors and not so with another, then there is a reason and this should be sought out and an assessment be made as to which results are the more credible. Econometricians are continually seeking ways of improving and refining estimation methods to deal with anomalies and biases. When more reliable methods are found, they tend to be integrated into the estimation procedures and modules found in the main software packages.

2.5 Concluding Remarks

The material on linear regression presented in Chapter 1 represents the basic knowledge required for estimating coefficients and testing hypotheses when the model used is linear. In this chapter, the use of the results obtained is emphasized using the much-used Oaxaca decomposition. The latter and developments thereof are particularly important tools in labour economics—they are in fact rarely used outside labour market contexts. The use of quantile regression has become widespread given the importance attached to distributional considerations in labour economics contexts. Quantile regression allows the practitioner to examine the relationship between variables and can also be used to undertake decompositions in the spirit of the Oaxaca approach. In the third section two key points were emphasized concerning the econometric analysis with panel data in labour economics. First, panel data enable the bias due to unobserved heterogeneity to be removed so long as that heterogeneity is time invariant. Second, fixed effects estimators solve the bias problem but prevent the estimation of the coefficients of variables that do not change over time. Finally, when the data are not randomly drawn from a population or when estimators with no analytical finite sample formula for the standard errors are used, care has to be taken. Several corrections are available in specific contexts and where these do not exist, simulation methods can be used.

Further Reading

The literature on decompositions is surveyed in Firpo, Fortin, and Lemieux (2010), although this is quite technical. Lemieux (2002) provides an accessible treatment of developments of the Oaxaca decomposition. Koenker's (2005) book is an important general reference on quantile regression and the article by Buchinsky (1998) provides a treatment that is particularly relevant for labour economics. A thorough presentation of econometric methods for panel data can be found in the microeconometrics texts by Wooldridge (2002) and Cameron and Trivedi (2005). More advanced treatments can be found in Arellano (2003), Baltagi (2008), and Matyas and Sevestre (2008). A very clear presentation of problems with different types of estimated standard error is Davidson and MacKinnon (1993). The same authors provide an excellent introduction to the bootstrap method (Davidson and MacKinnon, 2006) and Deaton (1996) covers issues related to clustering and intra-class correlations.

3

Dummy and Ordinal Dependent Variables

In many situations, the question addressed in labour economics is of a binary nature. An individual decides whether to participate or not in the labour force. He or she is either in or out. Sometimes, due to the way in which a survey is undertaken, data are only available for discrete binary outcomes—we do not know how many hours a person works, but we know that it is either part-time or full-time. In these circumstances, the variable that is being modelled is *dichotomous* and it is customary to treat such a variable as a dummy variable, sometimes referred to as a '(0,1)-dummy' or an indicator variable. In terms of the notation for the dependent variable (y_i) of the previous chapters, for each individual in the sample either $y_i = 0$ or $y_i = 1$. This type of data has given rise to the use of logit and probit models due to the discrete nature of the dependent variable. These are both nonlinear models and are estimated using maximum likelihood methods rather than by least squares. In this chapter we compare the results obtained by least squares and the logit/probit methods. We will also examine how these methods can be adapted for use with more than two alternatives. In the latter context, there is an important distinction to be made between ordered alternatives and straightforward, non-hierarchical multinomial outcomes.

3.1 The Linear Model and Least Squares Estimation

If the linear model is retained then $y_i = x_i'\beta + u_i$, where the right-hand side is a continuous function and the left-hand side is binary and therefore discrete. In other words, for any one of the explanatory variables, say x_{ki}, in the x_i' vector, the relationship between y and x_k will be a straight line while the observed data will be in separate groups—see Fig. 3.1. The estimated coefficient for this variable is an estimate of the slope of this straight line and it is not clear how this is to be interpreted since only two sample values can

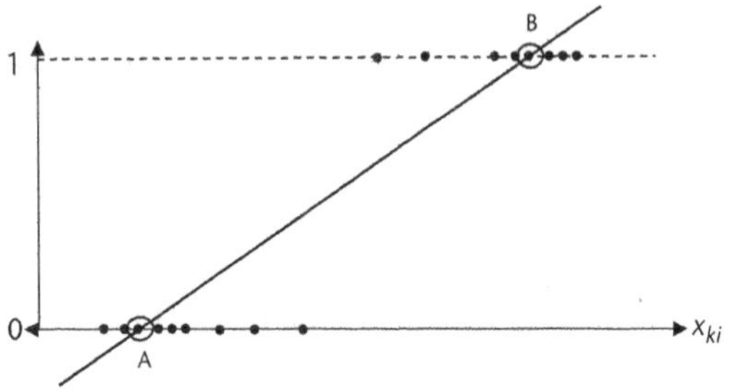

Figure 3.1. The linear model with a dummy dependent variable

be on this straight line (represented by points A and B). Since the relationship between y_i and x_{ki} is positive (by construction in this diagram), a higher value of x_k corresponds to a movement away from $y_i = 0$ and closer to $y_i = 1$. It is natural to interpret this in the following manner: the higher the value of x_k, the higher is the *probability* that $y_i = 1$ for given other characteristics x_i. This model is thus referred to as the *linear probability model*. The relationship can be expressed in terms of the conditional expectation:

$$E\left(y_i \,|x_i\right) = prob\left(y_i = 1 \mid x_i\right) = x_i'\beta \equiv p_i$$

This formulation poses no special problem as a model of how the probability changes with values of x, but there is no guarantee that the estimated parameters restrict the estimated probabilities for the whole sample to lie inside the (0,1) interval—the segments below A and above B in Fig. 3.1 are outside this interval but nevertheless correspond to values of x_{ki} contained in the sample. Given, however, that the mean probability will always lie inside the interval, it is possible in many cases to interpret the coefficients β as marginal effects for the average individual in the sample. In other words, if $\beta_k = 0.02$ and the average probability is 0.56, then a one unit increase in x_{ki} will result in an increase in the average probability of 2 percentage points to 0.58.

The coefficients can be estimated by least squares, although the binary nature of the dependent variable means that generalized least squares will be more efficient.[1] The least squares estimators of β will be unbiased if x_i is uncorrelated with u_i. If there is a constant term on the right-hand side, the average of the estimated probabilities ($\hat{p}_i = x_i'\hat{\beta}$) will be equal to the proportion of the sample for which $y_i = 1$ and the least squares residuals, $\hat{u}_i = y_i - \hat{p}_i$, will have zero mean. These residuals will be orthogonal to (uncorrelated with) each of the explanatory variables (x_{ki}) and, as a consequence, orthogonal to the estimated probabilities ($\hat{p}_i$). These

[1] The variance of the error term is given by $var\,(u_i) = x_i'\beta\,(1 - x_i'\beta)$ and this will not be constant across i.

latter properties are important in applications involving instrumental variables and two stage least squares when the endogenous variable is a dummy.

Consider the following model of female labour force participation in the United Kingdom. A sample of 3,371 women living in a couple is taken from the 2007 British Household Panel Survey (BHPS), 2,679 or 79.5% of whom are either in employment or unemployed. The vector of explanatory variables contains the number of children, a dummy variable representing the presence of young children under the age of 11, the number of years of post-compulsory education, health status (=1 if she is in good health), age and the extent of other income. The parameters of the linear probability model are presented in the first column of Table 3.1. Since the error term in the linear probability model is heteroscedastic, White standard errors are used. All coefficients are significantly different from zero at a 1% significance level. As the relationship is linear, the parameters are also the marginal

Table 3.1. Female labour force participation in the UK

Mean of dependent variable: 0.795, number of observations 3,371			
Explanatory variables (mean in parentheses)	Linear model*	Logit	Probit
Constant (1.00)	−0.125 (0.010)	−4.167 (0.64)	−2.371 (0.37)
Age (40.67)	0.043 (0.005)	0.277 (0.035)	0.158 (0.02)
Age squared (1765.5)	−0.00051 (0.00006)	−0.0034 (0.0004)	−0.0019 (0.0002)
Education (3.72)	0.026 (0.003)	0.176 (0.022)	0.099 (0.012)
Number of children under 16 (0.92)	−0.044 (0.013)	−0.256 (0.071)	−0.150 (0.041)
At least one aged under 11 (0.45)	−0.111 (0.024)	−0.921 (0.16)	−0.515 (0.091)
In good health (0.90)	0.132 (0.025)	0.771 (0.135)	0.500 (0.08)
Non-labour income (0.227 - £000s)	−0.15 (0.032)	−0.764 (0.12)	−0.430 (0.064)
Log likelihood	−1466.1	−1473.5	−1474.3
R^2/Pseudo R^2	0.144	0.138	0.139
Correct predictions:	19.1%	79.5%	79.5%
0 (692 obs)	85.7%	19.7%	19.4%
1 (2679 obs)	1.9%	96.7%	97.0%

*Heteroscedasticity consistent standard errors in parentheses

Source: author's calculations using data from the British Household Panel Survey

effects (except in the case of age, which appears as a quadratic function, and the two dummy variables).

There are two ways of interpreting the results. The first way is to examine how the probability of participation changes for a given individual when the explanatory variable changes. The second way is based on the notion of the conditional expectation. A change in an explanatory variable alters the average probability of labour force participation by an amount given by the marginal effect. This change is measured in *percentage points,* and since the average probability is simply the participation *rate,* the marginal effects can be interpreted as changes in the overall participation rate. Thus, one more year of post-compulsory education for everyone in the sample is estimated to increase the participation rate by 2.6 percentage points (from 79.5% to 82.1%). If a woman has another child (gives birth), her probability of participating in the labour force is reduced by 15.5 (= 0.044 + 0.111) percentage points. If she has a child who is currently aged 10, in the following year when her child is 11, her probability of participation increases by 11.1 points. As she passes from 30 to 31 years of age, her participation probability rises by 4 points (= 0.043–2 × 0.00051 × 30). For a woman aged 50, it increases by 3.8 points. Women in good health have on average a participation rate which is 13.2 points higher than those in poor health, other things being equal. Higher non-labour income reduces female labour force participation, which is line with the notion that non-market time (or 'leisure') is a normal good. One hundred pounds per month of additional non-labour income paid to all women in couples would reduce their overall participation rate by 1.5 percentage points.

As is often the case with linear models estimated with cross-section data on individuals, the R^2 is low. Finally, the estimated probability is greater than 1 for 5% of the sample and negative for only one observation. So it would appear that one of the key problems associated with the linear probability model is not too serious in this case. We return to this below.

3.2 Logit and Probit Models—A Common Set-up

The main alternatives to the linear probability model are the logit and probit models. These share a large number of features and, in practice, produce very similar results. They are also not that far removed from the linear model. Logit and probit models are simply nonlinear functions of the systematic component that appears in the linear model:[2]

$$prob\,(y_i = 1 \mid x_i) = F\,(x_i'\beta)$$

[2] The component $x_i'\beta$ is sometimes referred to as a 'linear index'.

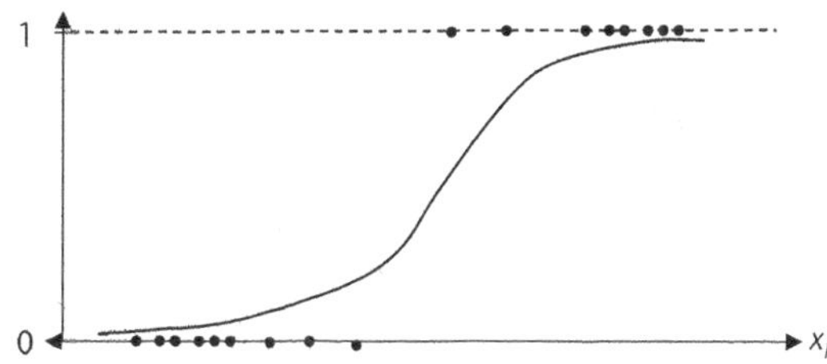

Figure 3.2. The logit/probit model

where $F(x_i'\beta)$ is a cumulative distribution function (CDF) and thus by definition $0 \leq F(x_i'\beta) \leq 1$.

These models guarantee that the estimated probability that $y_i = 1$ for any set of characteristics x_i lies between zero and one. When $F(x_i'\beta)$ is the CDF of the standard normal distribution, the model is a probit; when the CDF is for the logistic distribution, the model is a logit. For the same data as Fig. 3.1, the logit and probit models produce symmetric S-shaped or 'sigmoid' relationships between x_{ki} and $prob(y_i = 1 \mid x_i)$—see Fig. 3.2.

These models are, however, non-linear and cannot be transformed so as to be admissible for least squares estimation. Another consequence of this nonlinearity is that for a continuous explanatory variable, x_{ki}, the marginal effect is not constant. It is given by:

$$\frac{\partial F(x_i'\beta)}{\partial x_{ki}} = \beta_k f(x_i'\beta)$$

where $f(x_i'\beta)$ is the density function corresponding to the cumulative distribution function $F(x_i'\beta)$. The marginal effect takes the same sign as the coefficient, but is always smaller than the coefficient in absolute terms since $0 \leq f(x_i'\beta) \leq 1$. Unlike in the linear model, the marginal effect is not constant—it changes along the support of the distribution since the density changes. These features are common to both logit and probit models.

The specification of the two models can be derived from an underlying or latent model. The relationship between the linear model and these nonlinear models can be seen very clearly. The starting point is a linear model for a latent, unobservable variable y_i^*:

$$y_i^* = x_i'\beta + u_i$$

It is the choice of distribution for u_i that determines whether the model is a logit or probit. The latent variable can be interpreted sometimes as the difference between the utility levels associated with two choices. For example, if $U = V(y)$ is the utility from choosing option y, then the latent variable can be defined as:

$$y^* = V(y = 1) - V(y = 0)$$

A utility-maximizing individual faced with two options will choose $y = 1$ if $y^* > 0$ and $y = 0$ if $y^* \leq 0$. This difference in utilities[3] can be modelled as a function of a set of explanatory variables x_i. The probability model $prob\,(y_i = 1 \mid x_i) = F(x_i'\beta)$ can be derived as follows:

$$\begin{aligned} prob\,(y_i = 1 \mid x_i) &= prob\,(y_i^* > 0) = prob\,(x_i'\beta + u_i > 0) \\ &= prob\,(u_i > -x_i'\beta) = prob\,(u_i \leq x_i'\beta) \\ &= F(x_i'\beta) \end{aligned}$$

The equality in the second line applies because both the normal and logistic distributions are symmetric (and because the error term has zero mean).

3.2.1 *Estimation by Maximum Likelihood*

The logit and probit models are both nonlinear in their parameters and therefore least squares estimation is not possible. The standard approach is to use Fisher's maximum likelihood technique. This method involves making an *assumption* about the distribution of the data or the error term of the model, and then finding the parameters that maximize a function (the likelihood function) defined in terms of the total density of the sample. For a sample of n observations, the likelihood function is written as:

$$L = \prod_{i=1}^{n} f(y_i, x_i'\beta)$$

where $f(y_i, x_i'\beta)$ is the density function for the assumed distribution. The data are given and the unknowns are the parameters that characterize the distribution. In the case of dummy dependent variables, the density function is of the Bernouilli type:

$$f(y_i, x_i'\beta) = F(x_i'\beta) \text{ for } y_i = 1$$

$$f(y_i, x_i'\beta) = [1 - F(x_i'\beta)] \text{ for } y_i = 0$$

or putting the two together in a single expression:

$$f(y_i, x_i'\beta) = [F(x_i'\beta)]^{y_i} [1 - F(x_i'\beta)]^{1-y_i}$$

[3] If the utility functions are written as $V(y_i = j) = x_i'\beta_j + \varepsilon_i$, then

$$V(y_i = 1) - V(y_i = 0) = x_i'(\beta_1 - \beta_0) + \varepsilon_{1i} - \varepsilon_{0i} \quad = x_i'\beta + u_i$$

If ε_i follows a type 1 extreme error distribution, then u_i has a logistic distribution. This is referred to as the random utility model.

The means that the likelihood function can be written as:

$$L = \prod_{i=1}^{n} \left[F\left(x_i'\beta\right)\right]^{y_i} \left[1 - F\left(x_i'\beta\right)\right]^{1-y_i}$$

The function is maximized after conversion into natural logarithms. The first order conditions for maximization constitute a system of nonlinear equations and so the parameters that maximize the log likelihood have to be found by *iterative procedures*. The standard errors are calculated using the second derivatives of the log likelihood function. If the distributional assumption is justified and if certain regularity conditions hold, the maximum likelihood estimator will possess excellent asymptotic properties such as consistency, and will be the most efficient estimator (that is, have the smallest asymptotic variance).

3.2.2 *Hypothesis Testing*

Since asymptotically the maximum likelihood estimator has a normal distribution, hypothesis tests concerning individual coefficients can be undertaken using the *t*-ratio but using a critical value from the standard normal distribution (for a two-tailed test the critical values are 1.96 at a 5% significance level and 2.58 at the 1% level). For hypotheses containing more than one restriction, be they linear or nonlinear, the likelihood ratio (*LR*) test can be used. Like the *F* test, the model is estimated with and without the restrictions having been imposed, and the value of the log likelihood function in each case is obtained—call these LL_R and LL_U respectively. The *LR* statistic is:

$$LR = -2 \times (LL_R - LL_U)$$

The critical value for this test is taken from the χ^2 distribution where the number of degrees of freedom is equal to the number of restrictions in the null hypothesis. If the *LR* statistic is greater than the critical value then the hypothesis is rejected.

3.2.3 *Model Evaluation*

Given the binary nature of the dependent variable, the explanatory power of a logit or probit model can be assessed in terms of the predicted probability for each individual obtained from the model and the actual value of the binary variable. The predicted probability for individual *i* is given by:

$$\tilde{y}_i = F\left(x_i'\tilde{\beta}\right) \quad i = 1, 2, \ldots., n$$

where $\tilde{\beta}$ is the vector of parameter estimates obtained by maximum likelihood. The value of the dependent variable is either $y_i = 0$ or $y_i = 1$. The convention adopted for comparing predicted versus actual outcomes is the same as that applied when rounding numbers. This can equally be seen in terms of a cross tabulation, as in Fig. 3.3. A successful prediction is when $\tilde{y}_i \geq 0.5$ for individuals with $y_i = 1$ (in n_1^C cases), or when $\tilde{y}_i < 0.5$ coincides with $y_i = 0$ (in n_0^C cases). The combination $\tilde{y}_i \geq 0.5$ with for $y_i = 0$ individual i (in n_0^I cases) or when $\tilde{y}_i < 0.5$ coincides with $y_i = 1$ (in n_1^I cases) are considered bad predictions. The proportion of successful predictions is a measure of explanatory power—a little like the R^2 in a linear regression. The proportion of successful predictions is $\frac{n_0^C + n_1^C}{n}$. A danger that is sometimes encountered with this approach is when only a small proportion of the sample is in one of the binary categories, say $y_i = 1$. The model could have predicted very few (or even no) correct cases for this category (n_1 is small), but will have a high 'success' rate overall because n_0 is high.

The use of the threshold value of 0.5 would appear to be a natural choice in view of mathematical conventions for rounding numbers up. However, there is concern among certain practitioners that it is arbitrary and a better appreciation of the predictive performance of a model may be gained from calculating success rates using a lower figure, say 0.4, or to vary the threshold and examine how the success rate changes. An alternative method would be to divide the sample into cells defined by the explanatory variables and examine the success rate across cells.

An alternative approach to model evaluation is the calculation of a *pseudo-R^2*. The basic idea is that a model with no explanatory variables explains

	Predicted		
Observed	$\tilde{y}_i<0.5$	$\tilde{y}_i\geq0.5$	Proportion correct
$y_i=0$ (n_0 observations)	n_0^C	n_0^I	$\frac{n_0^C}{n_0}$
$y_i=1$ (n_1 observations)	n_1^I	n_1^C	$\frac{n_1^C}{n_1}$
	Overall proportion correct of correct predictions		$\frac{n_0^C+n_1^C}{n_0+n_1}$

Figure 3.3. The 'success' rate in logit and probit models

nothing. Call the value of the log likelihood for a model that contains only a constant term $\log L_0$. A model that explains a lot will have a much higher value for the log likelihood function $\log L_{\max}$. So while $\log L_0 < \log L_{\max}$, since these are both negative numbers their ratio is positive and $0 < \frac{\log L_{\max}}{\log L_0} < 1$. McFadden's pseudo-$R^2$ is defined as:

$$R_P^2 = 1 - \frac{\log L_{\max}}{\log L_0}$$

This statistic will take a value between zero and one, and is an indicator of the explanatory power of a given logit or probit model compared to one that contains only a constant term.

3.3 Interpreting the Output

Using the same data set, logit and probit model estimates of female labour force participation are presented in columns 3 and 4 of Table 3.1. It can be immediately seen that both models have identical signs for the coefficients—and, as pointed out above, the sign of the coefficient determines the sign of the marginal effect. Thus, the logit and probit models identify the same kind of effects as the linear probability model. Second, the t statistics are all more than three times the 5% critical value, and thus in both models all explanatory variables have significant coefficients. All of the explanatory variables have a statistically significant influence on the probability of participating in the labour force. These two conclusions are equivalent to saying that the results obtained using the logit and probit models are *qualititatively* the same (as are those obtained by the linear probability model).

For both models, the pseudo-R^2 is quite low in each case at around 0.13, although the proportion of correct predictions is high at 80%. These apparently contradictory figures have to be treated with some care. The pseudo-R^2 is not a comparison between actual and fitted values, as in the case of the R^2 in a linear regression. It resembles more the F statistic for the test of zero slope coefficients in a linear regression, and so is not a measure of the predictive ability of a model. The proportion of correct predictions combines in fact two 'success' rates in an arbitrary manner. For example, the percentage of correct predictions of being outside the labour force ($y_i = 0$) is only 20%. In other words, 80% of those women who do not participate have an estimated probability of participation of more than 0.5. The success rate for predicting participation ($y_i = 1$) is 97%. This is understandable because participants represent the vast majority of the sample (80%). The asymmetric performance of these models is hidden in the 'correct' predictions indicator.

In some applications, all the predictions are on one side, for example an estimated probability of 0.5 or more, with no predicted values below 0.5. This will show up in a reasonably satisfactory overall success rate if $y_i = 1$ for the majority of the sample.

3.3.1 *Marginal Effects*

The marginal effects are calculated differently for the two models. As pointed out above, the marginal effect of a continuous variable on the probability that $y_i = 1$ is that variable's coefficient multiplied by the value of the density function:

$$\frac{\partial F\left(x_i'\beta\right)}{\partial x_{ki}} = \beta_k f\left(x_i'\beta\right)$$

Since the density function changes with x_i the marginal effect is not constant across observations. As each model is based on a different probability distribution, the treatment of each model is different.

If the error term u_i has a normal distribution, the probit model is obtained so that

$$F\left(x_i'\beta\right) = \int_{-\infty}^{\frac{x_i'\beta}{\sigma}} \phi\left(v\right) dv$$

where $\phi\left(u\right)$ is the density function for the standard normal distribution,[4] that is when $u \sim N\left(0,\ 1\right)$. The marginal effect on the probability of a change in an explanatory variable in this case is:

$$\frac{\partial F\left(x_i'\beta\right)}{\partial x_{ki}} = \frac{\beta_k}{\sigma}\phi\left(\frac{x_i'\beta}{\sigma}\right)$$

This is generally evaluated at the means of the explanatory variables, $\bar{x}'$. The maximum value of the marginal effect occurs when $u = 0$ in $\phi\left(u\right)$ and—since $\phi\left(0\right) = \frac{1}{\sqrt{2\pi}} = 0.4$—is equal to

$$\frac{\partial F\left(x_i'\beta\right)}{\partial x_{ki}} = 0.4 \times \frac{\beta_k}{\sigma}$$

This provides an upper bound, and an easy way of getting an idea of the size of the marginal effects. Alternatively, for 50% of the sample the marginal effect will be between 0.3 and 0.4 times the coefficient (on the basis of the area under the density function for the standard normal distribution).

[4] $\phi\left(u\right) = \frac{1}{\sqrt{2\pi}} \exp\left(-\frac{1}{2}u^2\right)$

Returning to the probit model estimates in Table 3.1 (column 3), the continuous variables are education, age, and non-labour income. One more year of education will increase the probability of participation by at most 4 percentage points (0.4×0.099). Similarly, £1,000 more of non-labour income will reduce this probability by up to seventeen points (0.4 times $\times -0.43$). The effect of age is more difficult to calculate since the index function contains age and age squared. In this case, the derivative with respect to age is calculated and evaluated at a given age—say 40—which is close to the sample mean. The value of this derivative is $1.158 - 2 \times 0.0019 \times 40 = 0.006$. This derivative is the multiplied by the density evaluated again at the means of the explanatory variables—in this case $\phi\left(\frac{\bar{x}'\beta}{\sigma}\right) = 0.23$. The marginal effect of age is 0.0014 at the age of 40 for a woman with mean characteristics. For a woman aged 25, the calculation of this marginal effect would require entering an age of 25 in place of the mean and in the derivative calculation. Alternatively it can be said that this marginal effect would be at most

$$\left.\frac{\partial F(x_i'\beta)}{\partial age_i}\right|_{age=25} = 0.4 \times (0.158\text{-}2 \times 0.0019 \times 25) = 0.025$$

or an increase in the probability of participating of 2.5 points.

For dummy explanatory variables, care has to be taken when calculating marginal effects since the derivative of the function does not exist. For both logit and probit models in fact the marginal effect of a dummy variable x_{ji} (that is the effect of x_{ji} changing from zero to one) is obtained as:

$$\frac{\Delta F(x_i'\beta)}{\Delta x_{ji}} = F(x_i'\beta + \beta_j) - F(x_i'\beta)$$

In the probit model, a health shock which changes an individual's health status from good to bad means that the probability of participation goes from $F\left(\breve{x}'\tilde{\beta} + 0.50\right)$ to $F\left(\breve{x}'\tilde{\beta}\right)$ where $\breve{x}$ is the vector of means of all variables except health status. The estimated marginal effect is

$$\frac{\Delta F(x_i'\beta)}{\Delta health} = F(0.60) - F(1.10) = -0.139$$

and so a negative health shock reduces the probability by 14 percentage points. The same calculation for an additional (newly-born) child for a woman who already has one child aged 14, is a reduction of 17 points.

The logit model is obtained when the cumulative distribution function for the logistic distribution is used:

$$F(x_i'\beta) = \frac{\exp(x_i'\beta)}{1 + \exp(x_i'\beta)}$$

The marginal effect for a continuous variable in the logit model is

$$\frac{\partial F\left(x_i'\beta\right)}{\partial x_{ki}} = \beta_k \frac{\exp\left(x_i'\beta\right)}{\left[1+\exp\left(x_i'\beta\right)\right]^2} = \beta_k\, P_i\ [1-P_i]$$

where $P_i \equiv F\left(x_i'\beta\right) = prob\left(y_i = 1 \mid x_i\right)$. The maximum value of the marginal effect is obtained when $P_i = 0.5$ and $P_i\,(1-P_i) = 0.25$, so that:

$$\frac{\partial F\left(x_i'\beta\right)}{\partial x_{ki}} = 0.25\beta_k \tag{3.1}$$

When the estimated coefficients are scaled in this way in order to obtain the maximum marginal effects, there is very little difference in practice between the slopes of each of the functions. When the marginal effects are measured at the means of the x_i's, both will often be similar to the slope in the linear model.

For the logit model, the odds ratio is sometimes used in place of this marginal effect:

$$odds\ \ ratio = \frac{prob\left(y_i = 1\left|x_i, x_{ji} = 1\right.\right)}{prob\left(y_i = 1\left|x_i, x_{ji} = 0\right.\right)} = \exp\left(\beta_j\right)$$

This provides the ratio of probabilities that $y_i = 1$ with and without the characteristic represented by the dummy variable x_{ji}. If, for example, $\beta_j = 0.2$, then the probability that $y_i = 1$ for an individual for whom $x_{ji} = 1$ will be 22.1% higher ($\exp\left(\beta_j\right) = \exp(0.2) = 1.221$) than for an individual with identical characteristics except that $x_{ji} = 0$.

In the case of female labour force participation in the UK, the marginal effects for the logit model are similar to those obtained with the probit model. Thus an additional year of education increases the average probability of participation by 0.029 (= 0.176 × 0.795 x 0.205) or 2.9 percentage points. The maximum effect is 4.4 points, which is comparable with the maximum probit estimate of 4 points. Other marginal effects in the logit model are a 19 point reduction for £1,000 of extra non-labour income (17 points in the probit), a 0.1 point increase when passing from 40 to 41 years of age (probit 0.14), and a 2.7 point increase at the age of 25 (probit 2.5). These are all maximum possible values based on equation (3.1).

For two women, both with one child over 10, but one of whom has a baby, her participation probability will be 25 points lower (probit estimate: 17 points). Finally for health status, in the logit model the marginal effect of a health shock is estimated a reduction of 15.1 points:

$$\frac{\Delta F\left(x_i'\beta\right)}{\Delta health} = F(0.616) - F(1.387) = -0.151$$

The results are generally very similar and differences are partly due to the way in which marginal effects are calculated since a reference individual has to be defined. This can be someone with average characteristics except for the one that is changed, or someone with the average probability, or someone with characteristics corresponding to the modal value of the density in which case the maximum marginal effect is obtained. This ambiguity exists in these models because the relationship is nonlinear and so the marginal effect is not constant across the sample. An arbitrary choice of reference individual must be made. However, for explanatory variables in the linear index other than polynomial terms, the sign of the marginal effect and whether it is statistically different from zero can be determined without ambiguity. And in many empirical applications, this is all that the practitioner is interested in.

3.3.2 *Differences Between the Logit and Probit Models (and Linear Regression)*

Parameter estimation and the procedures for hypothesis testing using maximum likelihood are common to both the logit and probit models. However, one major difference between the models is that in the probit only $\frac{\beta}{\sigma}$ can be estimated—the value of the coefficients β cannot be separately identified. Practitioners often simply assume that $\sigma = 1$. In the light of these remarks, the presence of heteroscedasticity could have important consequences for the reliability of the estimates. For example, if there are distinct demographic or occupational groups in the sample, the variance of the error term may well differ across these groups. Imposing a common variance on the whole sample, as is the case in the probit model, will lead to inconsistent estimates of the parameters of interest $\frac{\beta}{\sigma}$. It is possible to take suspected heteroscedasticity[5] into account by assuming that the variance is given by a specific function of observables variables and incorporating this into the likelihood function. For example, if there is heteroscedasticity then $u_i \sim N(0, \sigma_i^2)$. Setting $\sigma_i^2 = \alpha_0 + \alpha_0 z_i^2$ means re-writing the probability that $y_i = 1$ as

$$\Pr(y_i = 1) = \Phi\left(\frac{x_i'\beta}{\sqrt{\alpha_0 + \alpha_1 z_i^2}}\right)$$

The difference between the logit and probit models is linked to the choice of distribution, a choice that is inherent in the use of the maximum likelihood method. The main difference in this context is in the thickness

[5] Davidson and MacKinnon (1993) propose a test of heteroscedasticity.

of the tails due to the higher variance of the logistic distribution.[6] While in practice there is very little difference between the values of the two cumulative distribution functions (CDFs) in the middle of the distribution, the logit model has a certain number of specific properties. First, it has the advantage of having a closed form for the CDF, whereas the CDF of the normal distribution requires the calculation of an integral. Estimation is not a problem due to the use of approximation functions, but the calculation of a probability for different individuals can be more cumbersome with the probit model. Second, if the model contains a constant, the first order conditions for maximum likelihood ensure that for the logit model the average predicted probability $\bar{\tilde{y}} = \frac{1}{n}\sum_{i=1}^{n} F\left(x_i'\tilde{\beta}\right)$ equals the sample average (that is the proportion for which $y_i = 1$ in the sample or $\bar{y} = \frac{1}{n}\sum_{i=1}^{n} y_i$). This is not the case in the probit model. This property is important when undertaking decompositions similar to that of Oaxaca with dummy dependent variables (see below).

In their recent book, *Mostly Harmless Econometrics* (2009) Joshua Angrist and Jorn-Steffen Pischke put forward a number of arguments in favour of using a linear regression with dummy dependent variables (the linear probability model) rather than one of these nonlinear models. The main point is that if the practitioner is only interested in the slope of the relation at the means of the explanatory variables, that is the marginal effects, the three models produce very similar results. Since the linear model possesses a large number of useful properties, no matter what the form of dependent variable, little is gained and a lot is lost by abandoning it for a nonlinear alternative. In particular, when an explanatory variable is a dummy and endogenous as well, using a linear regression in the first stage means that two stage least squares will possess all the appropriate properties for consistent estimation. Use of a nonlinear model such as the logit or probit in the first stage is a 'forbidden' regression and the second stage least squares estimates are inconsistent. Finally, the estimated parameters of the logit and probit models are not the 'parameters of interest' since a practitioner is usually interested in the marginal effects. The coefficients in the linear model are the marginal effects at the mean whereas, as pointed out above, in the logit and probit models, the marginal effects are the estimated coefficients multiplied by the density—and thus in order to calculate the marginal effect, a reference individual has to be defined.

The main weakness of the linear probability model arises when the practitioner is interested in the estimated probabilities. As well as the blatant matter of estimated probabilities falling outside the 0–1 interval, there is also the issue of correct predictions. In the female labour force application

[6] This variance is equal to $\frac{1}{3}\pi^2$.

presented above, the 'success' rate of the linear model is only 19% (compared to 80% for the nonlinear logit and probit models). Furthermore it is clear that in this application, the linear model only manages to correctly predict 1.9% of the actual participants—in other words for the 2,679 women in the sample who are economically active, the estimated probability obtained from linear model is less than 0.5 for 98% (2,625) of them. This is a badly performing model in this respect—in both absolute terms and relative to the logit and probit models.

3.3.3 *Decomposing Differences in Rates*

In the linear regression, differences in the mean of the dependent variable decompose in a straightforward and very useful manner using the Oaxaca approach. This is based on the fact that if there is a constant in a linear regression model[7] then the following equality is always true:

$$\bar{y} = \bar{x}'\hat{\beta}$$

Thus if a linear model is retained when the dependent variable is a dummy, the Oaxaca decomposition can be applied directly and the mean is simply the proportion in the sample for which $y_i = 1$, or in other words the *rate* (for example, participation rate, unemployment rate, and so on). However, the nonlinear nature of the logit and probit models means that such a decomposition cannot be undertaken in the same straightforward way. While for the logit model, if the model contains a constant the mean of the dependent variable can be expressed as:

$$\bar{y} = \frac{1}{n}\sum_{i=1}^{n} F\left(x_i'\tilde{\beta}\right)$$

where $\tilde{\beta}$ is the vector of parameters estimated by maximum likelihood, the average, $\bar{y}$, is not equal to $F\left(\bar{x}'\tilde{\beta}\right)$. For the probit model, neither equality holds. However, for the logit model, estimated separately for two groups (A and B), an Oaxaca-like decomposition can be obtained from the following identity:

$$\bar{y}_A - \bar{y}_B = \frac{1}{n_A}\sum_{i=1}^{n_A} F\left(x_{iA}'\tilde{\beta}_A\right) - \frac{1}{n_B}\sum_{i=1}^{n_B} F\left(x_{iB}'\tilde{\beta}_B\right)$$

$$= \left[\frac{1}{n_A}\sum_{i=1}^{n_A} F\left(x_{iA}'\tilde{\beta}_A\right) - \frac{1}{n_B}\sum_{i=1}^{n_B} F\left(x_{iB}'\tilde{\beta}_A\right)\right] + \left[\frac{1}{n_B}\sum_{i=1}^{n_B} F\left(x_{iB}'\tilde{\beta}_A\right) - \frac{1}{n_B}\sum_{i=1}^{n_B} F\left(x_{iB}'\tilde{\beta}_B\right)\right]$$

[7] The constant is the first element of the vector $\hat{\beta}$, and the first element of the vector $\bar{x}$ is one.

The first term represents the difference in rates due to characteristics while the second captures the effects of differences in coefficients. (Such a decomposition of the means is not generally valid for the probit model.) This aggregate decomposition is based on the creation of a counter-factual situation in order to isolate unexplained differences in the rates for the two groups. A detailed decomposition, whereby the contribution of each explanatory variable to the explanation of the differences in rates is calculated, can be obtained using a procedure proposed by Fairlie (2005).

Because of the nonlinear nature of the estimated models and the lack of correspondence between the conditional and unconditional means of the dependent variable in these models, a detailed decomposition is more complicated than in the linear framework. The first issue is that the sample sizes of the two groups will not be the same and a counter-factual has to be created by matching observations from the two groups. For example, assume that the linear index for group A is $x'_{iA}\tilde{\beta}_A = \tilde{\beta}_1^A + \tilde{\beta}_2^A x_{2i}^A + \tilde{\beta}_3^A x_{3i}^A$, and it is defined in the same manner for group B. Fairlie defines the contribution of variable say x_{3i} to the explained part of the differences as:

$$C_k = \frac{1}{n_B}\sum_{i=1}^{n_A}\left[F\left(\tilde{\beta}_1^P + \tilde{\beta}_2^P x_{2i}^A + \tilde{\beta}_3^P x_{3i}^A\right) - F\left(\tilde{\beta}_1^P + \tilde{\beta}_2^P x_{2i}^A + \tilde{\beta}_3^P x_{3i}^B\right)\right]$$

where $\tilde{\beta}_k^P$ is estimated by pooling the two samples and applying the logit approach. However, this calculation is a *pair-wise* comparison between the estimated probabilities and requires that there be as many values of $F\left(\tilde{\beta}_1^P + \tilde{\beta}_2^P x_{2i}^A + \tilde{\beta}_3^P x_{3i}^A\right)$ as there are of $F\left(\tilde{\beta}_1^P + \tilde{\beta}_2^P x_{2i}^A + \tilde{\beta}_3^P x_{3i}^B\right)$. Since this is highly unlikely in practice, it is necessary to simulate sample values by drawing sub-samples from the larger of the two groups. Suppose that $n_A > n_B$, then n_B values of x_{2i}^A and x_{3i}^A are required to make the comparison. Another complicating factor is that the contribution of each variable will depend on the order in which the decomposition is undertaken, that is which explanatory variable is the first chosen. The detailed decomposition is thus *path dependent.*

3.4 More Than Two Choices

In a labour market context, the choices available to an individual are often greater than two. A decision concerning participation in the labour force is not simply about working or not, but also between working full-time, part-time, or remaining outside the labour force. Other possibilities are working for an employer or on a self-employed basis, or on the basis of a type of contract (permanent, temporary) and not working at all. To the extent that an individual makes a choice out of a set of more than two possibilities, it is appropriate to model the factors that determine the choice made. Where there are several options on offer and the individual can choose only one, the appropriate econometric approach is through a multinomial model. In this section, we will first describe how to set up and use the multinomial logit model. When the choice available can be ordered in an ordinal hierarchical manner, an ordered probit model can be applied.

3.4.1 *Multinomial Logit*

Consider the case of the choice of labour market status—out of the labour force ($y_{1i} = 1$), work part-time ($y_{2i} = 1$), or work full-time ($y_{3i} = 1$). If someone is out of the labour force then $y_{2i} = 0$ and $y_{3i} = 0$, and the other dummies are defined in a similar, logical fashion. The multinomial logit, on the basis of latent decision-making rules, defines the probabilities of each of the outcomes as follows:

outside the labour force

$$\text{Prob}\left(y_{1i} = 1\,|x_i\right) = \frac{\exp\left(x_i'\beta_1\right)}{\exp\left(x_i'\beta_1\right) + \exp\left(x_i'\beta_2\right) + \exp\left(x_i'\beta_3\right)}$$

work part-time

$$\text{Prob}\left(y_{2i} = 1\,|x_i\right) = \frac{\exp\left(x_i'\beta_2\right)}{\exp\left(x_i'\beta_1\right) + \exp\left(x_i'\beta_2\right) + \exp\left(x_i'\beta_3\right)}$$

work full-time

$$\text{Prob}\left(y_{3i} = 1\,|x_i\right) = \frac{\exp\left(x_i'\beta_3\right)}{\exp\left(x_i'\beta_1\right) + \exp\left(x_i'\beta_2\right) + \exp\left(x_i'\beta_3\right)}$$

Clearly the three probabilities must sum to one (there are only three alternatives and one must be chosen). This means that one of the probabilities can be expressed in terms of the two others. In terms of the multinomial specification, this entails fixing all of the parameters in one of the vectors equal to zero. Since the choice is arbitrary, we set $\beta_1 = 0$, so that the probability that an individual chooses to remain outside the labour force becomes:

$$\text{Prob}\left(y_{1i} = 1\mid x_i\right) = \frac{1}{1 + \exp\left(x_i'\beta_2\right) + \exp\left(x_i'\beta_3\right)}$$

Note that the denominator has changed and will change in the same way in the specification of the other two probabilities. The parameters are estimated by maximum likelihood from the function by substituting in the formulae for the three probabilities:

$$L = \prod_{i=1}^{n} [\text{Prob}\,(y_{1i} = 1)]^{y_{1i}}\,[\text{Prob}\,(y_{2i} = 1)]^{y_{2i}}\,[\text{Prob}\,(y_{3i} = 1)]^{y_{3i}}$$

Thus the multinomial logit is a straightforward generalization of the binary logit model. Like the binary version, the estimated probabilities are constrained to lie between zero and one. The relationship between the probability of choosing any one of the possibilities and the explanatory variables is nonlinear and so the marginal effects are not constant. Furthermore, the presence of each explanatory variable in the denominator of the function defining the probabilities means that the marginal effect will have cross-status effects. For example, if an increase in non-labour income reduces labour force participation (that is raises the proportion outside of the labour force) it must reduce either part-time working or full-time working or both. For a continuous variable, x_{ki}, the marginal effect on the probability of choosing possibility j is given by:

$$\frac{\partial\, P\,(y_{ji} = 1 \mid x_i)}{\partial\, x_{ki}} = P_j \times \left[\beta_{jk} - \sum_{m=1}^{m=J} P_m \beta_{mk}\right]$$

where P_m is the proportion of the sample having chosen possibility m, and β_{mk} is the value of the coefficient on variable x_{ki} in the function for the probability of choosing possibility m (which is equal to zero for option $j = 1$ due to the normalization). The sign of the coefficient for a given possibility does not unambiguously determine the sign of the marginal effect on that probability. It is necessary to calculate the marginal effect using all the relevant parameters and the sample proportions in each category.

In the example of female labour force participation in the UK presented above, separating working women into part-time and full-time employees means that labour market choices can be analysed using a trinomial logit model. There is one thorny issue to be dealt with concerning labour force participation decisions at this point. In the binary case, the decision analysed was in or out of the labour force where 'in' means working or actively seeking work (unemployed). Once the hours status is introduced, the question arises as to what should be done with the unemployed. Being unemployed is not a status that is freely chosen, and thus does not fit into a multinomial *choice* framework. Because of this complication, the unemployed are omitted in the current application.

The percentages in the each of the three categories are inactive, 24.9%; part-time, 34.6%, and full-time, 40.3%. The parameter estimates, as mentioned above, do not unambiguously convey the signs of the marginal effects. Furthermore, the marginal effects are for each category, so that compared to a binary logit, the effects of the explanatory variables should have opposite signs for $\Pr(y_{1i} = 1)$(inactive) and $\Pr(y_{3i} = 1)$ (working full-time). The *marginal effects* and their estimated standard errors are presented in Table 3.2. The distinction between different types of labour force status provides a richer picture of the determinants of the choices made. For example, at a 5% level of significance, only three variables increase the probability of working part-time: age, the number of children, and the presence of young children. Education influences the probability of working full-time (positively) or being out of the labour force (negatively), but has no significant effect on working part-time (unless the significance level for the t test is increased). Non-labour income, as expected, increases the probability of remaining outside the labour force but has no impact on the probability of working part-time. Having a health problem has similar effects.

Apart from the choice of distribution for the probabilities, the multinomial logit model has one important property that could be a source of concern in empirical modelling. Since the probabilities are all defined in terms of a common denominator, the ratio of any two probabilities (the 'odds' ratio) is independent of the number of choices available. For example, in the part-time/full-time example, there are three options. If another possibility is added (for example, over-time working), this will not alter the odds ratios of the existing choices. In other words, the probability of choosing to work part-time compared to that of working full-time is unaffected by the inclusion of another possible status (working over-time) since:

Table 3.2. Multinomial logit marginal effects of the choice between inactivity, part-time work, and full-time work

	Estimated marginal effects		
Explanatory variables	Non-participation	Part-time work	Full-time work
Constant	0.996*	−0.626*	−0.371*
	(0.13)	(0.16)	(0.161)
Age	−0.053*	0.017*	0.036*
	(0.006)	(0.008)	(0.008)
Age squared	0.00066*	−0.00009*	−0.00056*
	(0.00008)	(0.0001)	(0.0001)
Education	−0.033*	−0.008*	0.041*
	(0.004)	(0.005)	(0.005)
Number of Children under 16	0.067*	0.077*	−0.138*
	(0.014)	(0.17)	(0.021)
At least one aged under 11	0.150*	0.117*	−0.266*
	(0.03)	(0.036)	(0.04)
In good health	−0.163*	0.038*	0.125*
	(0.026)	(0.036)	(0.04)
Non–labour income	0.221*	0.021*	−0.241*
	(0.03)	(0.04)	(0.05)

* indicates significant at 5%
Source: author's calculations using data from the British Household Panel Survey

$$\frac{\text{Prob}\,(y_{2i}=1)}{\text{Prob}\,(y_{3i}=1)} = \frac{\exp\,(x_i'\beta_2)}{\exp\,(x_i'\beta_3)} = \exp\,(x_i'\,(\beta_2-\beta_3))$$

This is called the *independence of irrelevant alternatives* condition (as in social choice theory), and imposes a certain structure on the model specification, namely, that the difference $(\beta_2 - \beta_3)$ is independent of whether there are three, four, or more alternatives available. This restriction may not be valid for the population being studied and will introduce bias if it is imposed arbitrarily.

A test of this restriction has been proposed by Hausman and McFadden (1984) and is essentially a comparison of two vectors of parameters (like the Hausman exogeneity test). In the above example, the vectors β_2 and β_3, each of which contain K parameters, are estimated with and without the fourth choice possibility (over-time working) along with their variance–covariance matrices (V_3 and V_4, respectively). Putting the parameters common to both models into one double-length vector of $2 \times K$ elements, call them $\tilde{\beta}^3$ and $\tilde{\beta}^4$ respectively, the hypothesis of the independence of irrelevant alternatives is rejected if the test statistic

$$HM = \left(\tilde{\beta}^3 - \tilde{\beta}^4\right)' \left[V^3 - V^4\right]^{-1} \left(\tilde{\beta}^3 - \tilde{\beta}^4\right)$$

is greater than the critical value obtained from the chi square distribution for $2 \times K$ degrees of freedom. If the hypothesis is rejected it is because the addition of an additional choice category has modified the parameters of the model. This should not occur when the multinomial specification is an adequate representation of the way in which individuals make their choices.

3.4.2 *The Ordered Probit Model*

An arguably more relevant model for the labour supply choices modelled here is an ordered model, since one way of treating the choice of labour market status is whether someone works more, less, or not at all. Part-time status tends to correspond to an arbitrary number of hours somewhere between zero and thirty. If individuals are categorized in one status or another on the basis of their hours of work, the choice between the three options can be modelled as an *ordered probit* model. The ordered probit model is based on a latent relationship in which the unobserved variable y_i^* is a function of a linear index $x_i'\beta$ and a normally distributed error term, u_i. Instead of defining a separate dummy variable for each status, we redefine the dependent variable as $y_i = 1,\ 2,\ 3$ for outside the labour force, working part-time, and working full-time respectively. In the ordered probit model, the hours intervals for each status are determined as parameters $(\alpha_1, \alpha_2, \ldots$.—

they are often called 'thresholds') and represent a constant term for each type of work status.

The probability that an individual chooses to be outside the labour force conditional on their characteristics is defined as:

$$\text{outside the labour force Prob}\left(y_i = 1\right) = \text{Prob}\left(y_i^* \leq \alpha_1\right)$$

For individuals who have chosen to work the relevant probabilities are:

$$\text{working part-time Prob}\left(y_i = 2\right) = \text{Prob}\left(\alpha_1 < y_i^* \leq \alpha_2\right)$$
$$\text{working full-time Prob}\left(y_i = 3\right) = \text{Prob}\left(\alpha_2 < y_i^*\right)$$

If the error term in the latent relationship is assumed to follow a standard normal distribution, each of these probabilities can be expressed in terms of the cumulative distribution function Prob $(u_i \leq z) = \Phi\,(z)$:

$$\begin{aligned}\text{Prob}\left(y_i = 1\right) &= \text{Prob}\left(y_i^* \leq \alpha_1\right) = \text{Prob}\left(x_i'\beta + u_i \leq \alpha_1\right)\\ &= \text{Prob}\left(u_i \leq \alpha_1 - x_i'\beta\right) = \Phi\left(\alpha_1 - x_i'\beta\right)\end{aligned}$$

Likewise the two other probabilities are defined as:

$$\text{Prob}\left(y_i = 2\right) = \text{Prob}\left(\alpha_1 < y_i^* \leq \alpha_2\right) = \Phi\left(\alpha_2 - x_i'\beta\right) - \Phi\left(\alpha_1 - x_i'\beta\right)$$
$$\text{Prob}\left(y_i = 3\right) = \text{Prob}\left(\alpha_2 < y_i^*\right) = 1 - \Phi\left(\alpha_2 - x_i'\beta\right)$$

The likelihood function has the same form as that of the multinomial logit model and is maximized with respect to α_1, α_2, and the vector β. There is no constant term in the vector β in this model since the threshold parameters play this role.

As with the multinomial logit model, the estimated parameters do not determine unambiguously the signs of the marginal effects of the variables. For example, the marginal effect of an increase in the continuous variable x_{ki} on the middle category is given by:

$$\frac{\partial P\left(y_i = 2\right)}{\partial x_{ki}} = \beta_k\left[\phi\left(\alpha_2 - x_i'\beta\right) - \phi\left(\alpha_1 - x_i'\beta\right)\right]$$

The difference in the values of the density function—the difference in square brackets—could be positive or negative, and so the marginal effect needs to be calculated for a specific value of the vector x_i. The marginal effects of the highest and lowest categories are unambiguously related to the sign of the coefficient β_k. Assuming that β_k is positive the marginal effects are:

$$\frac{\partial P(y_i = 1)}{\partial x_{ki}} = -\beta_k \phi \left(\alpha_1 - x_i'\beta\right) < 0$$

$$\frac{\partial P(y_i = 3)}{\partial x_{ki}} = \beta_k \phi \left(\alpha_2 - x_i'\beta\right) > 0$$

Thus the threshold parameters are not nuisance parameters. It is clear from the formulae above that they play a key role in the determination of the marginal effects.

3.5 Concluding Remarks

Binary discrete variables are very common in empirical labour economics since they are used to represent qualitative information such as an individual's status or choice. There is no natural numerical representation of such information. The objective of econometric analysis then becomes the investigation of the determinants of being in a given situation and this is modelled as a conditional probability. The issue being addressed is what is the probability that someone with a given set of characteristics chooses or finds themselves in a given situation, and how does this probability change when one or more of the characteristics are modified. Given that a probability must lie between zero and one, the econometric tools generally adopted are logit and probit type models. These are nonlinear models and are more difficult to use than a linear regression. The parameters are estimated by iterative search procedures rather than by applying a straightforward formula. The statistical properties of the estimators are asymptotic and the parameters of interest—the marginal effects—have to be calculated because they are not provided directly from the estimation procedure. Furthermore, the marginal effects are not constant across the population and have to be calculated for an arbitrarily chosen configuration of characteristics.

These specificities mean that a logit or probit model is more difficult to use than a linear regression. In recent years, the use of the linear probability model has become more common—in spite of its fundamental weakness that arises because the dependent variable on the left-hand side can only take two values (zero or one) and on the right-hand side there is a continuous, multi-valued linear component and continuous error term. The main argument advanced to justify this choice is that in empirical work the practitioner is not interested in the full range of predicted probabilities. What is important are the parameters of interest—the marginal effects for a typical individual. Unlike the logit and probit models, these are provided directly by ordinary least squares because the parameters of a linear regression are precisely the marginal effects. Furthermore, these tend to be close to what are obtained with the nonlinear models using mean characteristics. Coupled with the straightforward nature of estimation and a large number of well-known and analytic statistical properties, it is further argued by proponents of linear probability models that little useful extra information is obtained by changing over to a logit or probit model.

These arguments are quite persuasive, but they only apply when modelling a binary choice. Logit and probit models can be extended straightforwardly in order to analyse more than one choice. When extended to multinomial choices, the models become more complicated in terms of the estimation of the parameters and the determination of the marginal effects. There is no simple alternative via a linear regression in these cases. As in so many situations in empirical analysis, the practitioner has to make a decision based on the aims of his or her investigation and the nature of the data that are used.

Further Reading

The most widely cited text in this field is Maddala's (1983) book. Microeconometrics textbooks such as Wooldridge (2002) and Cameron and Trivedi (2005) provide more up-to-date treatments. An alternative approach to modelling binary choice variables is proposed by Angrist and Pischke (2009). Greene (2007) has substantial section on multinomial choice models.

4

Selectivity

One of the major concerns when modelling labour market behaviour and evaluating the consequences of policy measures, is that the individuals concerned do not constitute a random sample of the population. If people act on the basis of where they have a comparative advantage, they will self-select into particular jobs, occupations, or labour market programmes. Suppose for example that a firm provides free training on a voluntary basis to its workforce and what we are interested in knowing is what an individual (chosen at random) can be expected to gain from this training. It is probable, however, that those who stand to benefit most from the training will enrol, and those workers with little potential gain refrain. Those signing up for the training are therefore not a random sample of the workforce and the (average) gains from the programme will not be estimated in an unbiased manner when least squares techniques are used. Other common situations concern choice of labour market status. A single woman with young children will weigh up the costs and benefits of (a) paying for childcare and working for a wage, and (b) remaining outside of the labour force and caring for the children herself. Other things being equal, those women with higher potential market wages will be expected to choose to work. This means that a sample of working women used to estimate the return to human capital is not a random sample of the female population and the estimated parameters of the earnings equation may be biased.

The phenomenon of selectivity poses special difficulties for empirical analysis in labour economics. It creates a form of endogeneity whereby the variable of interest (the one that is being modelled) and one or more of its determinants are endogenous, with the same kind of consequences for the quality of estimates of parameters of interest as encountered in the standard regression framework. It is special because for some of the sample there are missing data—and this requires more sophisticated estimation methods than instrumental variables. As will be seen in this chapter, most of the approaches commonly used are based on the assumption that the error term has a normal distribution, and this may not always be compatible with the data.

4.1 A First Approach—Truncation Bias and a Pile-up of Zeros

Consider a data set in which individuals are only included if their monthly earnings fall below a certain level L (as in the study by Hausman and Wise, 1977). The density of the whole earnings distribution is therefore truncated at this point, and naturally the observed mean will be below the true mean (see Fig. 4.1). The return to human capital from this truncated sample estimated using OLS will be biased downwards since the mean or expectation of the error term conditional on earnings being below L is negative rather than zero (see Hausman and Wise, 1977). This is clear from Fig. 4.2.

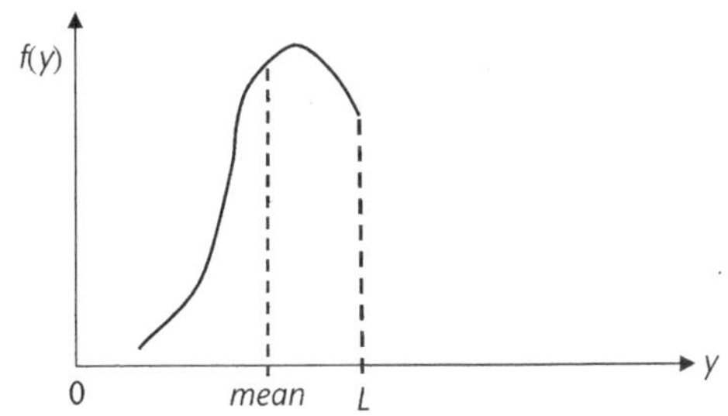

Figure 4.1. Distribution of a truncated variable

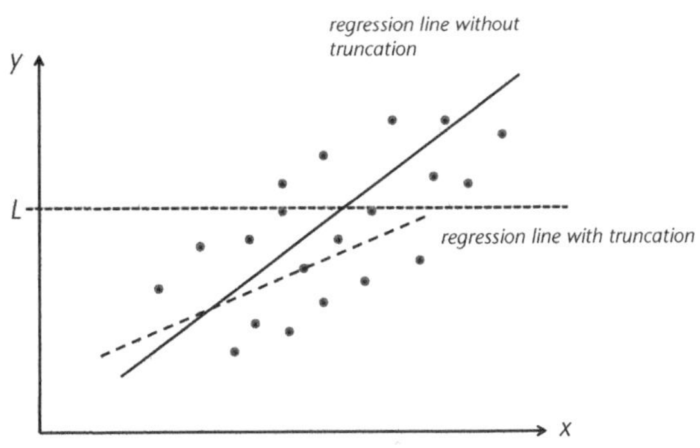

Figure 4.2. Regression when the dependent variable is truncated

In the absence of truncation, earnings (y_i) are determined as follows:

$$y_i = x_i'\beta + u_i \qquad u_i \sim N(0, \sigma^2)$$

where x_i is a vector of explanatory variables and β the vector of parameters of interest. While the latter are estimated by OLS, the same numerical values are obtained by applying maximum likelihood. For a sample of n independent observations, the likelihood function is given by:

$$L = \prod_{i=1}^{n} f(u_i) = \prod_{i=1}^{n} \frac{1}{\sqrt{2\pi\sigma^2}} \exp\left[-\frac{1}{2}\left(\frac{y_i - x_i'\beta}{\sigma}\right)^2\right]$$

This is transformed into logarithms:

$$\ln L = -\frac{n}{2}\ln 2\pi - \frac{n}{2}\ln \sigma^2 - \frac{1}{2}\sum_{i=1}^{n}\left(\frac{y_i - x_i'\beta}{\sigma}\right)^2$$

Maximizing the log likelihood function with respect to β is equivalent to minimizing $\sum_{i=1}^{n}(y_i - x_i'\beta)^2$ which is the same function that is minimized in order to obtain ordinary least squares estimates. This equivalence between OLS and maximum likelihood will be used as a basis for modifying the estimating technique when the data are truncated or censored.

In the case of truncation, the expectation of the error term when only individuals with earnings $y_i \leq L$ are included in the sample is given by:

$$E(u_i \mid y_i \leq L) = E(u_i \mid u_i \leq L - x_i'\beta) = -\sigma \frac{\phi\left(\frac{L - x_i'\beta}{\sigma}\right)}{\Phi\left(\frac{L - x_i'\beta}{\sigma}\right)} < 0$$

This and related formulae are obtained from properties of the normal distribution (derivations are provided in the Appendix to this chapter). If the error term does not follow a normal distribution then the formula does not apply. Since the upper part of the distribution is missing, it is clear that this conditional expectation will be negative (instead of zero), and so the OLS estimator of the parameters of interest will be biased and inconsistent. This is referred to as *truncation bias*. Hausman and Wise (1977) show that consistent estimates can be obtained using maximum likelihood methods. The log likelihood function simply contains an extra term compared to that arising when there is no truncation and is estimated for the truncated sample:

$$\ln L = -\frac{n}{2}\ln 2\pi - \frac{n}{2}\ln \sigma^2 - \frac{1}{2}\sum_{i=1}^{n}\left(\frac{y_i - x_i'\beta}{\sigma}\right)^2 - \sum_{i=1}^{n}\Phi\left(\frac{L - x_i'\beta}{\sigma}\right)$$

While truncation is sometimes present, it is less common than censoring. The data are censored when the dependent variable has a missing value for some

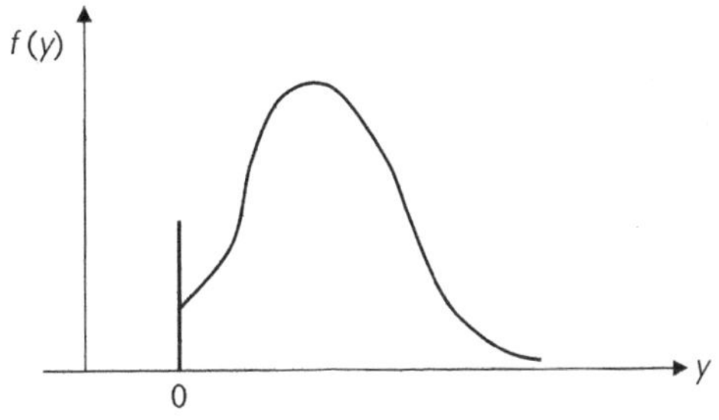

Figure 4.3. Distribution of a censored variable

members of the sample, but the explanatory variables are observed for all of the sample observations. Examples are missing earnings for people who do not work and top-coding earnings for highly paid individuals, so that we only know that the individual earns more than T but we do not know exactly how much. When there is censoring there is a piling up of sample observations at the censoring point (at zero earnings or earnings of T—see Fig. 4.3).

The first economist to examine this issue was James Tobin (1958) in the context of spending on durable goods. A household does not buy durable goods such as a washing machine every year so it records zero expenditure for some years. In a cross-section sample for a given year, a large proportion of households will have zero expenditure on washing machines. The 'Tobit' model is estimated by maximum likelihood using a similar log likelihood equation to that of Hausman and Wise, except that the sums are defined over different samples. In the zero expenditures example, the log likelihood function is given by:

$$\ln L = -\frac{n}{2}\ln 2\pi - \frac{n}{2}\ln\sigma^2 - \frac{1}{2}\sum_{y>0}\left(\frac{y_i - x_i'\beta}{\sigma}\right)^2 - \sum_{y=0}\Phi\left(\frac{-x_i'\beta}{\sigma}\right)$$

The Tobit model is basically 'half a regression' and 'half a probit': the regression part being the likelihood contribution of individuals with positive values for y_i, and the probit part the contribution of individuals for whom y_i is zero. In both the truncated and Tobit models, compared to the standard case, there is an extra term in the log likelihood function.

4.2 Sample Selection Bias—Missing Values

While the Tobit model takes into account the effect of censoring, it is not much used in its original form. The most common form of censoring is where the dependent variable y_i is observable if another variable takes a positive value. For example, earnings are observed only when hours of work are positive, that is when the individual has a job. This kind of situation has led to practitioners adopting a two equation model with a selection criterion:

$$y_{1i} = x_i'\beta + u_{1i} \qquad u_{1i} \sim N\left(0,\ \sigma_1^2\right)$$

$$y_{2i} = z_i'\gamma + u_{2i} \qquad u_{2i} \sim N\left(0,\ \sigma_2^2\right) \quad \operatorname{cov}\left(u_{1i}, u_{2i}\right) = \sigma_{12}$$

$$y_{1i} > 0 \quad \text{if} \quad y_{2i} > 0$$

otherwise y_{1i} is missing (the selection criterion) though x_i is observed.

The selection criterion is often treated in terms an unobserved, latent variable, y_{2i}^*, where $y_{2i}^* > 0$ implies that the observed value of y_{2i} is positive, and $y_{2i} = 0$ when $y_{2i}^* \leq 0$. In the case where the selection equation is defined in terms of a latent variable, it is generally assumed that $\sigma_2^2 = 1$.

In terms of the unbiased estimation of the parameter vector β, the key factor in this formulation will be the covariance between the two error terms, σ_{12}. If there is no selectivity phenomenon, OLS will not be biased (other things being equal). To see this, note that if the first equation is estimated solely with observations for which $y_{1i} > 0$, then the error term will have a non-zero expectation if $\sigma_{12} \neq 0$:

$$E\left(u_{1i} \,\middle|\, y_{2i} > 0\right) = E\left(u_{1i} \,\middle|\, u_{2i} > -z_i'\gamma\right) = \frac{\sigma_{12}}{\sigma_2^2} \frac{\phi\left(\frac{-z_i'\gamma}{\sigma}\right)}{1 - \Phi\left(\frac{-z_i'\gamma}{\sigma}\right)} \equiv \frac{\sigma_{12}}{\sigma_2^2}\lambda_i$$

(see the Appendix for a derivation). This special form for the conditional expectation again depends on the two error terms (u_i and v_i) having normal distributions. The term λ_i is variously referred to as the 'inverse Mills ratio', Heckman's lambda, and the hazard rate. The parameters $\frac{\sigma_{12}}{\sigma_2^2}$ can be expressed in terms of the correlation coefficient (ρ):

$$\frac{\sigma_{12}}{\sigma_2^2} = \rho\frac{\sigma_1}{\sigma_2} \quad \text{since} \quad \rho = \frac{\sigma_{12}}{\sigma_1\sigma_2}$$

When the normalization $\sigma_2 = 1$ is applied, this reduces to $\frac{\sigma_{12}}{\sigma_2^2} = \rho\sigma_1$. The parameters of interest, β, can be estimated using maximum likelihood. In the past, this task was often considered too complicated and above all took a long time to execute; nowadays it is in principle a straightforward application with current computer technology and software. In practice, due to the nature of the data, there may still be problems in obtaining the vector of parameters that maximizes the log likelihood function.

A popular alternative was proposed by James Heckman (1979). It is based on the idea that since the source of bias comes from the lambda term (λ_i) multiplied by a coefficient, the bias can be corrected by including λ_i in the regression equation for y_{1i} using only the observations for which $y_{1i} > 0$. If this term is explicitly included in the equation the remaining error term will have zero mean. Obviously λ_i depends on unknown parameters, but these can be replaced by parameters estimated by the probit method, since the probit directly estimates the ratio $\frac{\gamma}{\sigma_2}$ in the following equation:

$$\Pr\left(y_{2i} > 0\right) = 1 - \Phi\left(-\frac{z_i\gamma}{\sigma_2}\right) = \Phi\left(\frac{z_i\gamma}{\sigma_2}\right)$$

This is the first stage of Heckman's two stage estimator[1] and provides estimates of the coefficients in the vector $\frac{\gamma}{\sigma_2}$, which enables the lambda to be calculated as

$$\tilde{\lambda}_i = \frac{\phi\left(-z_i\frac{\tilde{\gamma}}{\sigma_2}\right)}{1 - \Phi\left(-z_i\frac{\tilde{\gamma}}{\sigma_2}\right)} = \frac{\phi\left(z_i\frac{\tilde{\gamma}}{\sigma_2}\right)}{\Phi\left(z_i\frac{\tilde{\gamma}}{\sigma_2}\right)}$$

The second equality is due to the symmetry of the normal distribution. The second stage of Heckman's approach involves estimating the following augmented regression by OLS

$$y_{1i} = x_i\beta + \theta\,\tilde{\lambda}_i + v_i \tag{4.1}$$

using only the observations for which $y_{1i} > 0$. By including this extra term, $\tilde{\lambda}_i$, the bias is removed from the estimation of the parameters of interest (strictly speaking, consistent estimates will be obtained because the additional term $\tilde{\lambda}_i$ has been estimated).

It is theoretically possible for the explanatory variables to be the same in both the selection equation and the outcome equation (that is the vectors are the same $x_i = z_i$). The parameters of the outcome equation are *identified* since λ_i is a nonlinear function. However, over a substantial range of values, λ_i is very close to a linear function of the index $z_i'\gamma$—notably in the range where $\frac{z_i'\gamma}{\sigma_2} < 0.5$—see Fig. 4.4. If $x_i = z_i$, then there can *in practice* be an identification problem due to multicollinearity. It is therefore advisable to examine the values of the estimated value of $\tilde{\lambda}_i$ in order to ensure that there are values outside of the linear range. A better strategy, in order to avoid the practical eventuality of collinearity between the two groups of variables, is to include at least one variable in z_i that is not in x_i, selected along the same lines as instrumental variables.

It has been strongly recommended by several authors that before proceeding with a fully parametric model of selectivity, it is important to undertake a test in order to establish whether there is in fact a problem. This test involves checking whether there is a correlation between the error terms of the two

[1] This is sometimes referred to as 'Heckman's lambda method' or the 'Heckit' method.

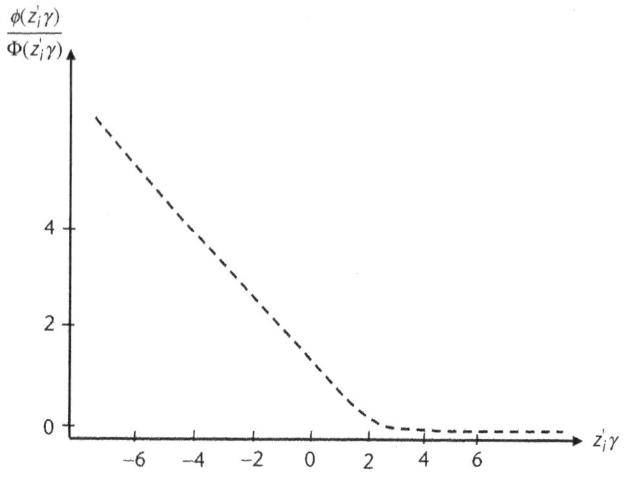

Figure 4.4. The inverse Mills ratio

equations, that is whether $\rho = 0$. Melino (1982) shows that (asymptotically) this is simply an asymptotic t test of the null hypothesis that $\theta = 0$ in equation (5.1). The statistic is the ratio of OLS estimates of the parameter and its standard error, and the statistic is compared to the critical value from the standard normal distribution (for example, there is no selectivity if the absolute value of the statistic is less than 1.96 at a 5% significance level).

If the selectivity is found, the OLS estimates of the parameters of equation (5.1) are consistent but the addition of an estimated term ($\tilde{\lambda}_i$) introduces heteroscedasticity and software packages calculate standard errors with correct formula. If one is doing the estimation manually using probit and OLS, White standard errors can be used (as suggested by Amemiya, 1985). The coefficient on the added term, $\tilde{\lambda}_i$, indicates the nature of the correlation between the error terms of the two equations (u_{1i} and u_{2i}), but the value of the coefficient (θ) is not restricted to lie between -1 and +1, since $\theta = \rho\sigma_1$ and only ρ is required to lie in this interval. If it is positive, then there is a positive relation between the unobserved factors that increase y_{1i} and those that increase y_{2i} (which increase the probability of having $y_{1i} > 0$).

The classic application of the sample selection model is female earnings. Given that the participation rate of women is significantly lower than that of males and the participation decision will depend on earnings potential, it is possible that the coefficients of the female earnings equation may be biased by the absence from the labour market of women who would otherwise have lower earnings. Using the same source of data for the UK as used in Chapter 3, the results for various models of female earnings are presented in Table 4.1.

Table 4.1. Female* earnings in the United Kingdom—is there sample selection bias?

	Ordinary least squares	Heckman's two stage method	Maximum likelihood estimates +	Probit model of participation
Number of observations	2,079	2,079	2,079	2,771
Explanatory variables:				
Constant	0.908 (0.127)	1.017 (0.133)	1.004 (0.151)	−2.684 (0.40)
Age	0.045 (0.007)	0.043 (0.0065)	0.043 (0.0073)	0.171 (0.022)
Age squared	−0.00049 (0.00008)	−0.00047 (0.00008)	−0.00047 (0.00009)	−0.0022 (0.0003)
Years of post-compulsory education	0.106 (0.004)	0.101 (0.0044)	0.101 (0.0044)	0.103 (0.013)
$\tilde{\lambda}_i$	–	−0.114 (0.042)	$\tilde{\rho}\tilde{\sigma}_1 = -0.101$ $\tilde{\rho} = -0.252$ (0.086) $\tilde{\sigma}_1 = 0.402$	–
Non-labour income	–	–	–	−0.639 (0.08)
Health status (=1 for good health)	–	–	–	0.534 (0.087)
Number of children aged under 18	–	–	–	−0.145 (0.045)
Presence of children aged under 11	–	–	–	−0.589 (0.098)
R^2/Log likelihood	0.278	0.280	−2332	−1301

*Females living in a couple + for the earnings equation only

Source: author's calculations using data from the British Household Panel Survey

As mentioned in Chapter 3, when analysing the status in the labour market of participants, there is a problem posed by the unemployed. They have decided to participate but have neither hours of work nor earnings. In the sample selection framework, as in the multinomial logit model, the unemployed are omitted from the analysis.

The sample size is thus reduced to 2,771 (from 3,371) once the unemployed are removed, and the employment participation rate is 75%. The sample selection model consists of two equations—a selection equation (modelled using a probit model) and an outcome equation (which is a linear model). There are two ways of estimating the model: maximum likelihood and the Heckman two stage method. Since the model is derived by assuming that the error terms in the participation and earnings equations both have normal distributions, maximum likelihood provides the most efficient (having the lowest variance) estimates. The Heckman approach is consistent and more straightforward to estimate. For a large sample the two approaches should produce similar results.

The probit estimates of participation are qualitatively the same as those obtained in Chapter 3, Table 3.1 for a full sample of labour force participants. Because the unemployed have been excluded here, there are some differences in the values of the coefficients. Women who work tend to be more highly educated, are in good health, have fewer children, do not have young children, and have little or no other sources of income. Interesting in the current context is the fact that the earnings equation specification (years of education and a quadratic function of age) has the expected effect on participation: women with higher potential earnings have a higher probability of participation. The same unobserved factors that increase the probability of participation also increase earnings. The outcome equation—the second stage in the Heckman approach—takes this into account. The parameter of interest is the correlation coefficient between the two error terms, ρ. This is estimated to negative ($\tilde{\rho} = -0.252$) and the Melino sample selection test indicates that sample selection bias is indeed present ($t = \frac{-0.114}{0.042} = -2.71$).

The problem detected means that OLS estimates of the coefficients of the earnings equations could be biased because of this selection mechanism. However, the returns to education and experience (proxied by age) are not very different from those obtained using a sample selection model. But the constant term is underestimated by OLS suggesting that, for given characteristics, participants have higher *potential* earnings than non-participants, which is consistent with the negative selectivity bias detected.

4.3 Marginal Effects and Oaxaca Decompositions in Selectivity Models

While in theoretical terms the Heckman approach is less appealing given that maximum likelihood is feasible (and is necessarily more efficient), the introduction of the lambda term is useful for interpreting the marginal effects of the variables in this model. The presence of lambda in the equation means that the marginal effect of any variable (x_{ki}) that appears both in the selection equation (for y_{2i}) and in the outcome equation (for y_{1i}) will not be constant. Essentially, an increase in x_{ki} will change the probability that $y_{1i} > 0$ and will also change the value y_{1i} for those for whom y_{1i} is already positive. The marginal effect of an increase of x_{ki} on y_{1i} is a weighted sum of these two effects.

The actual calculation is a little complicated because of the conditional nature of the outcome equation—it is estimated solely for those with $y_{1i} > 0$.

In order to obtain the formula for the marginal effect of a continuous explanatory variable on the outcome variable, y_{1i}, it is necessary to determine the equation for the *unconditional* (with respect to $y_{2i} > 0$) mean of y_{1i} which is given by (see the Appendix for details):

$$E\left(y_{1i} \mid x_i\right) = \Phi\left(z_i'\gamma\right) \times E\left(y_{1i} \mid x_{2i},\, y_{2i} > 0\right)$$
$$= \Phi\left(z_i'\gamma\right) \times x_i'\beta + \rho\sigma_1 \times \phi\left(z_i'\gamma\right)$$

An explanatory variable—x_{ki}—that appears in both sets of explanatory variables (in x_i and in z_i) will have a marginal effect on y_{1i} given by:

$$\frac{\partial E\left(y_{1i} \mid x_i\right)}{\partial x_{ki}} = \beta_k \times \Phi\left(z_i'\gamma\right) + \gamma_k \times \phi\left(z_i'\gamma\right) \times \left[x_i'\beta - \rho\sigma_1 z_i'\gamma\right]$$

The marginal effect is not given by β_k as in a linear regression. This is another indication of the importance of sample selection bias. The marginal effect is calculated by using the estimated parameters from equation (5.1) and inserting the mean values of x_i and z_i from the whole sample. Most software packages calculate these directly. However, for the same reasons as in less complicated models, the marginal effect of a dummy variable should be treated as a discrete change since it involves a comparison of two situations:

$$\Delta_k = E\left(y_{1i} \mid x_i,\, x_{ki} = 1\right) - E\left(y_{1i} \mid x_i,\, x_{ki} = 0\right)$$

The Oaxaca decomposition can be extended to incorporate selectivity but this raises some important questions of which decomposition we are trying to calculate. From an econometric standpoint, if the only issue at hand is to use reliable estimates of the returns to characteristics (the β's) in the decomposition, then the selectivity term is not relevant—it is included in the equation simply to purge the estimation process of bias. This may be the case in earnings comparisons for different ethnic groups with different employment prospects. The mean-based, aggregate decomposition will contain an additional residual since the Oaxaca decomposition is exact only if standard OLS estimates from an equation containing a constant are used. In other words, if $\hat{\beta}_H$ is the vector of estimated coefficients from the Heckman procedure then we obtain a mean of $\tilde{y}_1 = \frac{1}{n}\sum_{i=1}^{n} x_i'\,\hat{\beta}_H \neq \bar{y}_1$. While if there is a constant term in the model, the average fitted value is equal to the unconditional mean of y_{1i}:

$$\frac{1}{n}\sum_{i=1}^{n} \hat{y}_{1i} = \frac{1}{n}\sum_{i=1}^{n}\left(x_i'\hat{\beta}_H + \hat{\theta}\,\tilde{\lambda}_i\right) = \bar{y}_1$$

The decomposition into explained and unexplained components can always be undertaken by defining a counter-factual group, but there is no guarantee that if the coefficients were identical for the groups under comparison (the definition of discrimination in this context) that the decomposition would register zero discrimination once differences in characteristics have been taken into account. An exact decomposition is possible if the selectivity corrected earnings are used:

$$y_i^S \equiv y_{1i} - \hat{\theta}\,\tilde{\lambda}_i = x_i'\hat{\beta}_H + \hat{v}_i$$

In this estimated model, the residual ($\hat{v}_i$) will have a zero mean and so the decomposition of mean differences in the left-hand side variable will be exact:

$$\bar{y}^{SM} - \bar{y}^{SF} = \left(\bar{x}^M - \bar{x}^F\right)' \hat{\beta}_H^M + \bar{x}^{F\prime}\left(\hat{\beta}_H^M - \hat{\beta}_H^F\right)$$

There are two limitations associated with this approach. First, it does not provide a decomposition of *observed* earnings differences and second, and linked to this, there are situations where the selectivity mechanism may be particularly important, such as in the analysis of gender differences in earnings. For example, in most countries females have significantly lower labour force participation rates than males. If participation is at all related to earnings potential, then earnings equations will be contaminated by selectivity bias (this is similar to selectivity on the basis of comparative advantage addressed in the next section). If this bias is 'corrected' for using a Heckman-type approach, then the decomposition of earnings differences into explained and unexplained components has to be modified. Essentially, the selection equation contains all or a subset of the explanatory variables found in the outcome equation. Factors that influence participation also determine earnings and thus could be treated as an additional component in the decomposition of group differences in average earnings.

$$\bar{y}^M - \bar{y}^F = \left(\bar{x}^M - \bar{x}^F\right)' \hat{\beta}_H^M + \bar{x}^{F\prime}\left(\hat{\beta}_H^M - \hat{\beta}_H^F\right) + \left(\hat{\theta}^M\bar{\lambda}^M - \hat{\theta}^F\bar{\lambda}^F\right)$$

Neuman and Oaxaca (2004) examine different interpretations of the selectivity component. For example, is the selectivity equation that determines the inverse Mills ratios the same for males and females and if not is this due to market discrimination or societal factors that determine gender roles? Put differently, should all or part of the final term in this decomposition be in the explained part or the discrimination component? The answer to these questions depends on the objectives of the study and the theoretical basis for the analysis.

4.4 The Roy Model—The Role of Comparative Advantage

In the above models, the issue was whether the observed outcome variable was subject to sample selection: that is, whether y_i (Tobit) or y_{1i} (Heckman) is zero or missing for some members of the sample. These are special cases of a more general approach to selectivity that is often referred to as the *Roy model*. The latter in fact was a theoretical economic model that showed that because of comparative advantage, workers seeking the maximum gain would self-select into different occupations. Since comparative advantage—over and above characteristics such as education and experience—is unobserved, observed earnings differentials cannot be attributed solely to human capital differences, and any attempt to quantify the impact of education and experience on earnings differences will be confounded by selectivity bias.

Consider the following situation where a worker is looking for a job and in the labour market there are two types of job vacancy: those proposed by firms in which earnings are determined by wage bargaining with unions, and those in firms in which pay is determined by individual productivity. Calling the logarithm of earnings in each type of firm y_i^U and y_i^N, respectively, there are two earnings functions:

$$y_i^U = x_i^U \beta^U + u_i^U$$
$$y_i^N = x_i^N \beta^N + u_i^N$$

The model is completed with a selection equation:

$$S_i^* = z_i' \gamma + u_i^*$$

where $S_i^* > 0$ means the worker chooses a union job ($y_i^U > 0$ and y_i^N is missing) and if $S_i^* \leq 0$ he or she chooses a non-union job (so that $y_i^N > 0$ and y_i^U is missing). The explanatory variables in the selection equation z_i contain the explanatory variables in the earnings equations plus additional non-wage factors that influence job choice.

Using the same reasoning as before, the self-selection mechanism means that the error terms in the earnings equations, conditional on the value of S_i^*, will not have zero expectations. As before, we assume that the three error terms follow a joint normal distribution with zero (unconditional) means, respective variances of σ_U^2, σ_N^2 and $\sigma_S^2 (= 1)$, and correlation coefficients ρ_{US} and ρ_{NS} (which can be used to define the covariances). Using the similar derivations to those above (the details are in the Appendix), the conditional expectations of the error terms in the earnings equations are:

$$E\left(u_i^U \mid S_i^* > 0\right) = E\left(u_i^U \mid u_i^* > -z_i'\gamma\right) = \rho_{US}\sigma_U \frac{\phi\left(z_i'\gamma\right)}{\Phi\left(z_i'\gamma\right)}$$

and

$$E\left(u_i^N \mid S_i^* \leq 0\right) = E\left(u_i^N \mid u_i^* \leq -z_i'\gamma\right) = -\rho_{NS}\sigma_N \frac{\phi\left(z_i'\gamma\right)}{1-\Phi\left(z_i'\gamma\right)}$$

Estimation of either earnings equation by least squares using only positive values of earnings will yield biased and inconsistent estimates if the error term of the equation is correlated with the error term of the selection equation—in other words, if $\rho_{US} \neq 0$ and/or $\rho_{NS} \neq 0$. These correlation coefficients themselves can be negative or positive, but should be of opposite sign. If unobserved factors that increase the probability of accepting a non-union job (dynamism, ambition, and career progression) are positively correlated with the error term of the earnings equation, then $\rho_{NS} > 0$. The same factors would be expected to be negatively correlated with the error term in the union earnings equation, where earnings are determined more by collective and equity objectives.

As with the Heckman lambda method, a two stage estimator (as in equation 4.1 above with the appropriate correction factor $\lambda_i^U = \frac{\phi(z_i'\gamma)}{\Phi(z_i'\gamma)}$ or $\lambda_i^N = \frac{\phi(z_i'\gamma)}{1-\Phi(z_i'\gamma)}$) will provide consistent estimates. First a probit model is estimated, and the two correction terms are generated. These are then included as additional regressors in their respective equations, and OLS is applied separately to each of the following models for the two sub-samples:

$$y_i^U = x_i^U\beta^U + \theta^U\tilde{\lambda}_i^U + v_i^U \text{ for union members}$$

$$y_i^N = x_i^N\beta^N + \theta^N\tilde{\lambda}_i^N + v_i^N \text{ for non-union members}$$

The estimated standard errors will need to take into account the fact that the inverse Mills ratios ($\tilde{\lambda}_i^U$ and $\tilde{\lambda}_i^N$) have been estimated using probit estimates. Alternatively, maximum likelihood estimation is now relatively straightforward in this case. The return to union membership is then calculated using the Oaxaca approach (but ignoring the correction factors) for identical characteristics.

In the 1999 Current Population Survey data used in Chapters 1 and 2, there is information on whether an individual is a union member or not. Confining the sample to males for whom all the relevant variables are recorded, there are 36,853 observations of which 7,766 or 21% are union members. If a dummy variable representing union membership is included in the standard Mincer earnings equation (see Table 4.2, column 1), the estimated premium to union membership is 25.1% (= (exp(0.224) − 1) × 100%). The Roy model suggests that those with a comparative advantage in union jobs will move there and those who will obtain higher wages without unions seek non-union employment. The latter are probably those who will obtain higher returns to their human capital and other productive capacities. By estimating separate equations for union members and non-union individuals, the sorting mechanism identified in the Roy framework is modelled using a probit equation. Other than years of education and a quadratic function of experience, the explanatory variables in the probit equation are marital status, the presence of children, and living in a large city. The number of children has no effect on the probability of union membership, while married men and those living cities have a higher rate of union membership.

These probit estimates can now be used to generate the terms $\tilde{\lambda}_i^U$ and $\tilde{\lambda}_i^N$ for union members and non-members, respectively, for separate equations are estimated in order to see whether the selection mechanism has an effect on the estimated returns to human capital and union membership. The estimated parameters for the union equation are presented in column 3 of Table 4.2. First, the coefficient on the selectivity term is significantly

Table 4.2. The effect of unions on male earnings—a Roy model for the United States

Dependent variable: log of hourly earnings				
	Ordinary least squares	Probit model of union membership	Union equation	Non-union equation
Number of observations	36,853	36,853	7,766	29,087
Explanatory variables:				
Constant	5.743 (0.014)	−1.912 (0.057)	6.970 (0.093)	5.721 (0.016)
Experience	0.042 (0.0007)	0.050 (0.003)	0.020 (0.0027)	0.026 (0.001)
Experience squared	−0.00078 (0.00002)	−0.00063 (0.00008)	−0.00043 (0.00006)	−0.00065 (0.0003)
Years of education	0.068 (0.001)	0.209 (0.004)	0.046 (0.0026)	0.061 (0.0013)
Union member	0.224 (0.005)	–	–	–
City	–	0.252 (0.015)	–	–
Married	–	0.173 (0.017)	–	–
Number of children	–	0.033*ns* (0.031)	–	–
$\tilde{\lambda}_i$	–		$\tilde{\rho}_{UE}\sigma_U = -0.368$ (0.039)	$\tilde{\rho}_{NE}\sigma_N = -0.884$ (0.037)
R^2/Log likelihood	0.300	-17 855	0.149	0.275

'ns' indicates not significant

Source: author's calculations using data from the Merged Outgoing Rotation Group of the Current Population Survey, 1999

different from zero: there is a selection mechanism at work. Second, the returns to education and experience are both lower than in the equation for the pooled sample. It would appear that an additional year of education increases earnings by only 4.7% (compared to 7%) and the 11th year of experience gives an increase of 1.1% (compared to 2.7%). The constant term, however, is substantially higher. For the non-union equation, the selectivity term is highly significant and confirms that a selection mechanism operates. The coefficients of the equation indicate that the returns to human capital are higher than for union members—a return to education of 6.3% and to the 11th year of experience 1.3%. However, the constant term is much lower.

The effect of union membership on earnings in the presence of selectivity can be estimated by calculating the counter-factual earnings for a union member, that is what he would have earned in the non-union sector. Using the non-union coefficients with the average union characteristics gives average counter-factual log earnings of 6.698:

$$\begin{aligned}\bar{y}^C &= 5.721 + 0.0256 \times \exp - 0.00065 \times \exp^2 + 0.061 \times \text{educ} \\ &= 5.721 + 0.0256 \times 20 - 0.00065 \times 486.56 + 0.061 \times 12.89\end{aligned}$$

The average earnings of a union member in the sample is 7.292 and so the return to membership is 81% ((exp(7.292 − 76.698) − 1) × 100%). This is a very large estimated effect and there are good reasons to believe it to be an over-estimate (in particular the relatively poor specification of the probit model to determine membership and the restrictiveness of the strict Mincer earnings equation). Nevertheless it is larger than the effect estimated assuming no selectivity, and this is an interesting conclusion.

4.5 The Normality Assumption

All of the approaches presented in this chapter are based on models in which the error terms are assumed to follow a normal distribution. The different formulae for the selectivity biases are derived for this distributional assumption, and the estimation methods—maximum likelihood or corrected least squares using a control function—require that this assumption is valid in order to provide consistent estimates. As is always the case in econometrics, it is a good idea to test the validity of a hypothesis rather than simply assume that it is true. Failing this, it is worth examining the robustness of the results under different assumptions. There are semi-parametric and non-parametric approaches that can be used (these are not presented here because of their complexity, although see Vella, 1998 for a clear presentation).

There exist tests of the hypothesis that an error term in the equations follows a normal distribution. In the sample selection model with bivariate normally distributed errors and estimated using the Heckman approach, one method of testing whether the assumption of a normal distribution is valid is to add $(z_i\tilde{\gamma}) \times \tilde{\lambda}_i$ and $(z_i\tilde{\gamma})^2 \times \tilde{\lambda}_i$ to the second stage regression:

$$y_{1i} = x_i\beta + \theta\,\tilde{\lambda}_i + \alpha_1\left((z_i\tilde{\gamma}) \times \tilde{\lambda}\right) + \alpha_2\left((z_i\tilde{\gamma})^2 \times \tilde{\lambda}\right) + \eta_i$$

where η_i is the error term when the equation is modified in this way. If the joint hypothesis $H_0 : \alpha_1 = \alpha_2 = 0$ is rejected then the normality assumption is not appropriate. Using the standard F statistic, F*, for these two restrictions, the statistic $2 \times F^*$ is compared to the critical value in the Chi square distribution for 2 degrees of freedom. Therefore, at a 5% significance level, if the statistic is greater than 5.99, the null hypothesis is rejected. This test was suggested by Bera, Jarque, and Lee (1984) and is applied in this form by Vella (1998).

4.6 Concluding Remarks

Selection mechanisms and the bias they introduce into econometric estimation constitute one of the principal concerns in empirical labour economics. Economic behaviour is based to a large extent on incentives and the existence of comparative advantage. This means that individuals' labour force participation, job choice, enrolment in the labour market, and educational programmes and mobility will all be influenced by the potential gains that exist (or are thought to exist). People self-select into different situations and types of status. The econometric approaches presented in this chapter were developed by econometricians specifically to analyse these features of labour market behaviour.

The major worry associated with these methods, as stressed in the last section, is that the models are constructed on the basis that the unobserved characteristics and factors captured by the error terms are normally distributed. If this is not the case then the econometric approach is not valid and may produce very unreliable results. As is usually the case in econometrics when a weakness or constraint is identified, research is undertaken to find alternative methods or ways of attenuating the consequences of misspecification through transformations and preliminary testing. Much of current research is aimed developing non-parametric techniques and these are beginning to represent feasible alternatives.

Further Reading

Amemiya (1985) and Maddala (1983) are the classic references on selectivity. The book by Pudney (1989) provides a detailed treatment and many extensions of the methods presented here. Heckman's articles (1979) and (1990) provide insights into the key issues. The survey by Vella (1998) contains details of non parametric methods.

Appendix

1. The conditional expectation of the error term under truncation

The expected value of the error term in the absence of truncation is given by:

$$E(u_i) = \int_{-\infty}^{\infty} u\, f(u)\, du$$

where $f(u_i)$ is the density function for the error term or the *unconditional* density. The density function in the presence of truncation, illustrated in Fig. 4.1, is given by the *conditional* density:

$$f\left(u_i \,|\, y_i \leq L\right) = \frac{f(u)}{pr\left(y_i \leq L\right)}$$

The denominator ensures that the integral of the conditional density is equal to one (as is always the case with the integral of a density function be it conditional or unconditional).

The expected value of the error term in the presence of truncation is then given by:

$$E\left(u_i \,|\, y_i \leq L\right) = E\left(u_i \,|\, u_i \leq L - x_i'\beta\right) = \frac{\int_{-\infty}^{L-x_i'\beta} u\, f(u)\, du}{pr\left(y_i \leq L\right)}$$

The numerator is the standard formula for determining the expected value (except for the limits of the integral).

For reasons that will become apparent, u_i is assumed to have a normal distribution $u_i \sim N\left(0, \sigma^2\right)$. The density function in this case is:

$$f(u_i) = \frac{1}{\sqrt{2\pi\sigma^2}} \exp\left[-\frac{1}{2}\left(\frac{u_i}{\sigma}\right)^2\right]$$

The conditional expectation of the error term can be expressed in terms of the density (ϕ) and cumulative distribution (Φ) functions for the standard normal distribution (mean zero and unit variance) where for $v_i = \frac{u_i}{\sigma} \sim N(0,\ 1)$:

$$\phi\left(v_i\right) = \frac{1}{\sqrt{2\pi}} \exp\left[-\frac{1}{2} v_i^2\right]$$

The integral in the numerator can be expressed in terms of $v_i = \frac{u_i}{\sigma}$, by replacing u_i by v_i, du_i by $\sigma\ dv_i$, and by modifying the limits of the integral:

$$E\left(u_i \mid y_i \leq L\right) = \sigma \frac{\int_{-\infty}^{\frac{L - x_i'\beta}{\sigma}} v\,\phi\left(v\right)\,dv}{\Phi\left(\frac{L - x_i'\beta}{\sigma}\right)}$$

This expression can be simplified by noting that in the case of the density of the standard normal distribution, $\phi'\left(v\right) = \frac{\partial\phi(v)}{\partial v} = -v\,\phi\left(v\right)$ and $\phi\left(-\infty\right) = \phi\left(+\infty\right) = 0$, so that

$$E\left(u_i \mid y_i \leq L\right) = -\sigma \frac{\int_{-\infty}^{\frac{L - x_i'\beta}{\sigma}} \phi'\left(v\right)\,dv}{\Phi\left(\frac{L - x_i'\beta}{\sigma}\right)} = -\sigma \frac{\phi\left(\frac{L - x_i'\beta}{\sigma}\right) - \phi\left(-\infty\right)}{\Phi\left(\frac{L - x_i'\beta}{\sigma}\right)}$$

$$= -\sigma \frac{\phi\left(\frac{L - x_i'\beta}{\sigma}\right)}{\Phi\left(\frac{L - x_i'\beta}{\sigma}\right)} < 0$$

2. The conditional expectation of the error term with sample selection

When there are two equations and the error terms are jointly normally distributed:

$$\begin{pmatrix} u_{1i} \\ u_{2i} \end{pmatrix} \sim N\left[\begin{pmatrix} 0 \\ 0 \end{pmatrix}, \begin{pmatrix} \sigma_1^2 & \sigma_{12} \\ \sigma_{12} & \sigma_2^2 \end{pmatrix}\right]$$

the expectation of u_{1i} conditional on being selected into the sample ($y_{2i} > 0$) is:

$$E\left(u_{1i} \mid y_{2i} > 0\right) = E\left(u_{1i} \mid u_{2i} > -z_i'\gamma\right) = \frac{\sigma_{12}}{\sigma_2^2} \frac{\sigma_2 \int_{-z_i'\gamma}^{\infty} v\,\phi\left(v\right)\,dv}{\Pr\left(y_{2i} > 0\right)}$$

$$= \frac{\sigma_{12}}{\sigma_2^2} \frac{\sigma_2 \int_{-z_i'\gamma}^{\infty} v\,\phi\left(v\right)\,dv}{1 - \Phi\left(\frac{-z_i'\gamma}{\sigma_2}\right)}$$

Using the property $\phi'\left(v\right) = -v\,\phi\left(v\right)$ and recalling that $\phi\left(+\infty\right) = 0$, the conditional expectation becomes:

$$E\left(u_{1i} \mid y_{2i} > 0\right) = -\frac{\sigma_{12}}{\sigma_2^2}\,\frac{\sigma_2 \dfrac{\int_{-z_i'\gamma}^{\infty} \phi'(v)\, dv}{}}{1-\Phi\left(\dfrac{-z_i'\gamma}{\sigma_2}\right)} = -\frac{\sigma_{12}}{\sigma_2^2}\,\frac{\phi(\infty)-\phi\left(\dfrac{-z_i'\gamma}{\sigma_2}\right)}{1-\Phi\left(\dfrac{-z_i'\gamma}{\sigma_2}\right)} \tag{A.4.1}$$

$$= \frac{\sigma_{12}}{\sigma_2^2}\,\frac{\phi\left(\dfrac{-z_i'\gamma}{\sigma_2}\right)}{1-\Phi\left(\dfrac{-z_i'\gamma}{\sigma_2}\right)} \equiv \frac{\sigma_{12}}{\sigma_2^2}\lambda_i$$

Since the standard normal distribution is symmetric around zero, we can also write:

$$\lambda_i = \frac{\phi\left(\frac{z_i'\gamma}{\sigma_2}\right)}{\Phi\left(\frac{z_i'\gamma}{\sigma_2}\right)}$$

3. Marginal effects in the sample selection model

The marginal effects are determined in the equation for the outcome variable but not conditional on selection. In other words we need to use $E\left(y_{1i} \mid x_i\right)$ and not what was estimated, $E\left(y_{1i} \mid x_{2i}, y_{2i} > 0\right)$. The relevant conditional expectation is:

$$E\left(y_{1i} \mid x_i\right) = \text{Prob}\left(y_{2i} \le 0\right) \times 0 + \text{Prob}\left(y_{2i} > 0\right) \times E\left(y_{1i} \mid x_{2i}, y_{2i} > 0\right)$$

The first part on the right-hand side is for those with no observed value for y_{1i} and who were selected out. The second term corresponds to those 'selected in'. Both terms are weighted by the probability of being selected in or out, as is normal when determining expected values. The first term on the right-hand side is zero and so after substituting $\text{Prob}\left(y_{2i} > 0\right) = \Phi\left(z_i'\gamma\right)$ and $E\left(y_{1i} \mid x_{2i}, y_{2i} > 0\right) = x_i\beta + \theta\,\tilde{\lambda}_i$, the relevant formula for determining marginal effects is given by:

$$E\left(y_{1i} \mid x_i\right) = \Phi\left(z_i'\gamma\right) \times x_i'\beta + \rho\sigma_1 \times \phi\left(z_i'\gamma\right)$$

where $\Phi\left(z_i'\gamma\right) \times \lambda_i = \phi\left(z_i'\gamma\right)$ from the definition of λ_i.

The explanatory variable under scrutiny, x_{ki}, is assumed to be an element present in each of the vectors x_i' and z_i'. The marginal effect on y_{1i} of an increase in x_{ki} is given by the partial derivative of the expected value:

$$\frac{\partial E\left(y_{1i} \mid x_i\right)}{\partial x_{ki}} = \gamma_k\,\phi\left(z_i'\gamma\right) \times x_i'\beta + \Phi\left(z_i'\gamma\right) \times \beta_k - \gamma_k \times \rho\sigma_1 \times z_i'\gamma \times \phi\left(z_i'\gamma\right)$$

where $\dfrac{\partial\,\phi\left(z_i'\gamma\right)}{\partial\,x_i} = -\gamma_k \times z_i'\gamma \times \phi\left(z_i'\gamma\right)$ from the property $\phi'(v) = -v\,\phi(v)$.

4. The conditional expectation of the error terms in two equations with selectivity bias

The three error terms assumed to be normally distributed as follows:

$$\begin{pmatrix} u_i^U \\ u_i^N \\ u_i^* \end{pmatrix} \sim N\left[\begin{pmatrix} 0 \\ 0 \\ 0 \end{pmatrix}, \begin{pmatrix} \sigma_U^2 & \sigma_{UN} & \sigma_{US} \\ \sigma_{UN} & \sigma_N^2 & \sigma_{NS} \\ \sigma_{US} & \sigma_{NS} & 1 \end{pmatrix}\right]$$

The derivation of conditional expectation $E\left(u_i^U \mid S_i^* > 0\right)$ is exactly the same as in equation (A.4.1) above for the Heckman approach and is given by:

$$E\left(u_i^U \mid S_i^* > 0\right) = \sigma_{US}\frac{\phi\left(-z_i'\gamma\right)}{1 - \Phi\left(-z_i'\gamma\right)} = \rho_{US}\sigma_S\frac{\phi\left(-z_i'\gamma\right)}{\Phi\left(-z_i'\gamma\right)}$$

The case where $S_i^* \leq 0$ is found in a similar way:

$$E\left(u_i^N \mid S_i^* \leq 0\right) = E\left(u_i^N \mid u_i^* \leq -z_i'\gamma\right) = \frac{\sigma_{NS}}{\sigma_S^2}\frac{\int_{-\infty}^{-z_i'\gamma} v\phi(v)\, dv}{\text{Prob}\left(u_i^* \leq -z_i'\gamma\right)}$$

$$= -\sigma_{NS}\frac{\int_{-\infty}^{-z_i'\gamma} \phi'(v)\, dv}{\Phi\left(-z_i'\gamma\right)}$$

$$= -\sigma_{NS}\frac{\phi\left(-z_i'\gamma\right) - \phi(-\infty)}{1 - \Phi\left(z_i'\gamma\right)} = -\rho_{NS}\sigma_N\frac{\phi\left(z_i'\gamma\right)}{1 - \Phi\left(z_i'\gamma\right)}$$

Both conditional expectations are expressed in terms of the inverse Mills ratio and a correlation coefficient. A key feature in the derivations is the sign of these terms.

5

Duration Models

In many countries, the rise and persistence of unemployment from the 1970s onwards led to labour economists paying special attention to the *duration* of a spell of unemployment. There are two reasons for this. First, at the macroeconomic level, it became clear that unemployment was not rising as a result of increasing numbers of people entering unemployment due to lay-offs and increased labour force participation. In other words, there did not appear to have been a substantial increase in the inflow rate into unemployment. If the unemployment rate remained high, it was more to do with people remaining unemployed for longer periods. Second, there has been more focus on microeconomic aspects of unemployment and, in particular, why certain individuals appeared to encounter difficulties in leaving unemployment. The analysis of the determinants of the length of unemployment spells is largely based on individual data.

The econometric analysis of spell durations is based on methods developed in other disciplines (especially biometrics and the analysis of survival times after surgery or medical treatment). Furthermore, while the focus was initially on unemployment duration, other issues in labour economics can be approached in a similar manner, such as job mobility, strike duration, and time out of the labour force for maternity leave. Essentially, the aim is to determine the factors that influence the length of a spell in a given state, and the likelihood of leaving that state for another. In this chapter for reasons of clarity the material will be presented in terms of unemployment durations.

The econometric (and more generally statistical) analysis of the length of a spell requires a different approach from the standard practice. In order to get to an unemployment duration of, say, six months, an individual must have already been in that state for five months. This trivial statement has important consequences for the modelling of the determinants of the length of a spell. For example, if at a given point in time—1 May 2010—there are 2 million persons unemployed, and by the following month 100,000 of these had left unemployment, one might be tempted to use a dummy dependent variable model (logit or probit or even linear probability) to determine the relative importance of different characteristics for the probability of leaving unemployment before 1 June . However, the individuals unemployed on 1 May 2010 have been there for different lengths of time—some as little as a week, others more than three years. The chances of leaving unemployment in a given month will depend on the time already spent unemployed—a phenomenon called duration dependence. The relevant approach in this case is where this probability of leaving the state is modelled as *conditional* on being unemployed for a given time. Furthermore, among those unemployed at given time, the distribution of durations is biased by the presence of those less likely to leave unemployment having longer durations while the more employable will have already disappeared from the stock of unemployed persons. This is called *length-biased sampling* because short spells are under-sampled and so the stock of persons unemployed is not a representative sample of persons experiencing unemployment. A third issue is that if we are interested in what determines the length of a spell of unemployment, we need to know what determines the *completed* duration. We will normally know what this is for the 100,000 who leave the ranks of the unemployed in June 2010, but the 1.9 million who remain will all have incomplete durations. In the language of Tobit-type models, the variable of interest is (right) *censored*. Least squares estimation of the parameters of a linear model with completed and incomplete durations will generally be biased and inconsistent.

The type of model to be used, and the accompanying estimation method, will depend on the form of data that are available. The *ideal form* for analysing unemployment durations is where a group of n individuals all become unemployed at the same time (say t_0), and these individuals are followed through time until they each have left unemployment. This would be case A in Fig. 5.1. Once the last person has left, the data for the n completed durations are analysed in order to identify the factors that give rise to longer (completed) spells of unemployment. In the first part of this chapter, we will examine methods for analysing data on completed durations. A particularity of econometric duration analysis is that the various statistical tools that are used have mainly been borrowed from other disciplines. These are outlined in the first section and the links between them are spelt out. Two principal methods are presented for analysing a sample which has these 'ideal' features. These models serve as benchmarks which can be adapted for modelling with less ideal forms of data.

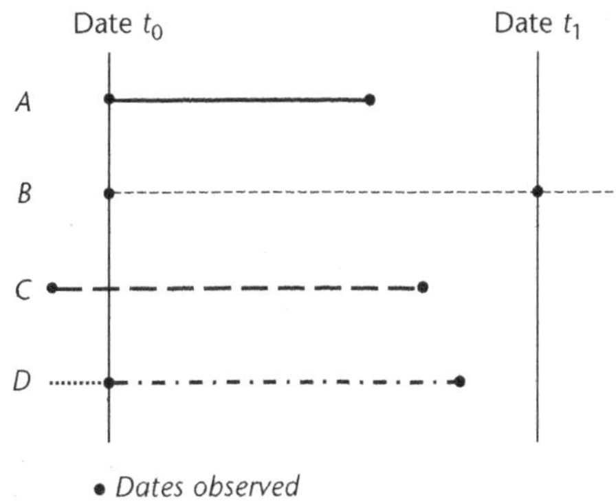

Figure 5.1. Types of duration data

While some data sets on completed durations exist for unemployment, the majority will have censored durations for at least part of the sample. For example, in many European countries, it is not uncommon for certain individuals to remain unemployed for more than three years, and so the data on completed durations for one month's inflow will not be usable for some time. This corresponds to case B in Fig. 5.1 where the individual is not observed after date t_1. Furthermore, in practice, the size of a sample of persons entering unemployment in a given week in many countries tends to be relatively small. Typically, the labour force surveys undertaken in European countries use a cross-section of the whole population of working age, only a small minority of which is unemployed at the time of the survey. There are retrospective questions concerning previous employment and the date at which the person entered unemployment, illustrated as case C in Fig. 5.1. For these persons the uncompleted, and therefore censored, duration can be determined at date t_0. In a subsequent interview at date t_1, say, the same sample of persons is asked about their new status, if any. (Sometimes the actual date of entry into unemployment cannot be determined or the date indicated may not be reliable, as in case D.)

Among those unemployed at the time of the first survey, some will have left unemployment and will have completed durations. It is this form of data, with a mixture of completed and incomplete spells, that is typically used to analyse unemployment durations. In the second section of this chapter, the practicalities of duration modelling are addressed. In the final section, we address issues of how to treat duration dependence (whereby the probability of leaving unemployment changes with the spell length, notably for the long term unemployed) and unobserved factors that influence the time spent in a labour market state.

5.1 Analysing Completed Durations

There are a number of concepts and definitions that need to be presented before describing models appropriate for duration analysis. The key idea is that a person enters a state (in a labour market context, unemployment, inactivity, employment) and remains there for a period—a duration which we call t_i for individual i—and then exits to another state. In order for a spell to be a completed duration, transition to another state is necessary. Thus analysis can proceed in terms of durations themselves or in terms of transitions, and the two are necessarily linked.

A key concept used in analysing durations is the *survivor function*, which measures the proportion of individuals still present in a state (who have 'survived') after a specific duration (t). This can also be expressed as the probability that for an individual drawn at random from the population under scrutiny, his or her duration in that state will be greater than t. Using the notion of a cumulative distribution function, $\mathrm{F}(t)$, the survivor function is defined by:

$$S(t) = \mathrm{Prob}\,(t_i > t) = 1 - \mathrm{F}\,(t) \quad \text{for} \quad t = 0,\ 1, \ldots,\ T$$

where $S(0) = 1$ and $S(T) = 0$. The survivor function has the form presented in Fig. 5.2(a).

The mean (or expected) duration is the integral of this survivor function over the range of durations $[0, T]$—see Appendix for the derivation:

$$E(t) = \int_0^T S(t)\,dt$$

Clearly, the cumulative distribution function of durations can be obtained trivially from the survivor function:

$$F(t) = \mathrm{Prob}(t_i \leq t) = 1 - S\,(t)$$

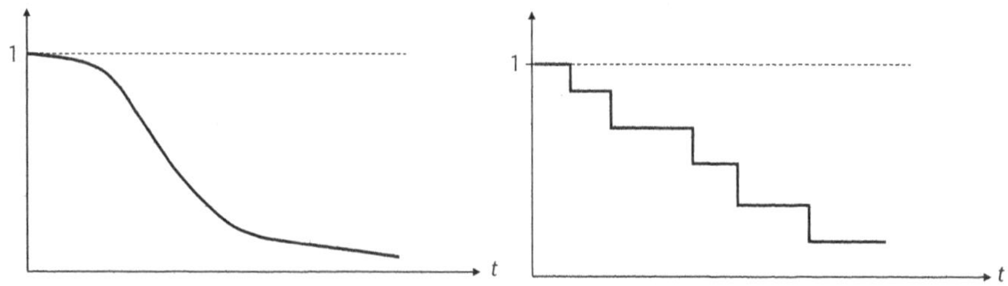

(a) Continous data

(b) Discrete data

Figure 5.2. The survivor function

The corresponding density function is obtained by differentiation:

$$f(t) = \frac{\partial F(t)}{\partial t} = -\frac{\partial S(t)}{\partial t} \tag{5.1}$$

The density and the survivor functions are used to define a key concept which is widely used when analysing durations in labour economics, the *hazard rate*. The hazard function measures the prospect of leaving unemployment in period t—having been unemployed up to that point:

$$\lambda(t) = \frac{f(t)}{S(t)} \qquad \lambda(t) \geq 0$$

This is not, strictly-speaking, a probability[1] since, in theory, when defined as a function of continuous time, the hazard rate can be greater than 1. These different ways of representing data on durations are very closely linked.[2] Knowledge of one is sufficient for knowledge of all of the others. These relationships hold for 'continuous time', whereas in practice data are generally available in weeks, months, and years rather than on a second-by-second basis. This requires that certain manipulations need to be treated carefully when using continuous time concepts with samples of discrete time data.

A useful starting point when using duration data is to obtain the graph of the survivor function or the hazard function using a non-parametric technique. By looking at how the probability of leaving a state (such as unemployment) changes with duration, important insights can be gained into how to model the determinants of spell lengths. As an example, consider a sample of n individuals each of whom has completed a spell of unemployment ($t_i > 0$), where the longest spell is of length T. The estimate of value of the survivor function at each duration t, for $t = 0, 1, \ldots, T$, is given by:

$$\hat{S}(t) = 1 - \frac{1}{n}\sum_{j=0}^{t} d_j = \frac{1}{n}\sum_{j=t+1}^{T} d_j$$

where d_j is the number leaving the state after a stay of j months. For discrete duration data, the survivor function will be a step-wise linear downward sloping function of time as in Fig. 5.2(b).

[1] Formally, the hazard rate is defined as: $\lambda(t) = \lim_{\Delta t \to 0} \frac{\text{prob}\ (t < t_i \leq t + \Delta t \mid t_i > t)}{\Delta t}$

[2] A related concept is the *integrated hazard* function which is often useful in linking the different concepts—see Appendix.

5.2 Econometric Modelling of Spell Lengths

While for unemployment, data on completed durations only are likely to be uncommon, for certain phenomena, for example strikes and time out of the labour force for maternity leave, it is possible to have a data set where all durations have terminated (due to a transition out of that state). However, given that models become increasingly complicated as the data on durations are censored, have missing values, or are measured with error, it is useful to begin by considering situations where all durations have been completed. This will allow us to see the extent to which a regression approach can used. There are three main approaches to modelling durations in a given labour market state: (i) estimation of a distribution of spell lengths (a non-parametric approach); (ii) a model of the determinants of the length of a spell (called accelerated life models); and (iii) modelling the determinants of the probability of leaving a state (hazard models).

5.2.1 *A Linear Regression Model of Durations*

Consider as a first approach the following model of what determines the length of a spell, t_i, for individual i:

$$t_i = g\,(x_i; \beta; \varepsilon_i)$$

for explanatory variables[3] x_i, parameters β, and an error term ε_i. A first issue is that a duration cannot be negative, and it is common practice to transform this variable into logarithms, for example:

$$\log t_i = x_i'\beta + \varepsilon_i$$

This is called the *accelerated failure time model.* The coefficients of the right-hand side variables will therefore be interpreted in terms of the proportionate effect of a variable on the length of a spell. In fact, as noted in the context of earnings equations, if an explanatory variable x_k increases by one unit, the duration of the spell will increase by $[\exp(\beta_k) - 1] \times 100\%$.

While it is possible to estimate the parameters β by least squares, these are not the only parameters of interest. Any model of spell length must at a minimum allow for the possibility that the hazard rate changes with the length of time already spent in a state. Using the duration of a spell on the left-hand side then means that the distribution of the error term will determine the shape of the hazard for a typical individual, and this

[3] Sometimes these are referred to as 'covariates', as in the biostatistical literature.

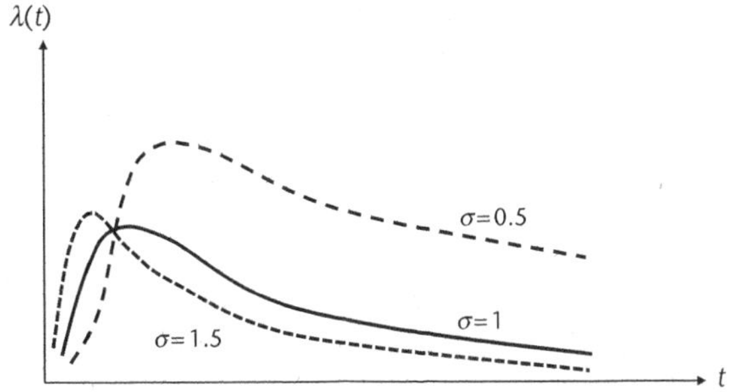

Figure 5.3. Hazard shapes for the accelerated time failure model with a log normally distributed error term

requires an assumption to be made about the distribution. If ε_i has a normal distribution, then duration will be log normally distributed:

$$\log t_i \sim N\left(x_i'\beta,\ \sigma^2\right).$$

For a given vector of characteristics, x, the value of σ will determine the shape of the hazard function, and a number of cases are shown in Fig. 5.3. The hazard is increasing and then decreasing in each case and thus, when the lognormal distribution is assumed, the hazard will be *non-monotonic*. When the error term follows a normal distribution, OLS will identify all of the parameters of interest and will be equivalent to maximum likelihood.

When the relevant distribution is non-normal, maximum likelihood can be used directly using the assumed density, $f(\varepsilon_i)$, to form the likelihood function:

$$L = \prod_{i=1}^{n} f\left(\varepsilon_i\right) = \prod_{i=1}^{n} f\left(\log t_i - x_i'\beta\right)$$

5.2.2 *Modelling the Hazard Rate Rather than the Spell Length*

In labour economics applications, a more common approach to analysing the factors influencing spell lengths is to model the determinants of the hazard rate, that is the prospect of leaving unemployment conditional on having been unemployed up to that point in time. The difference between using duration as the left-hand side variable and the hazard rate, is that the latter will depend explicitly on time spent in the state. A functional form for this duration dependence will be need to be specified. A typical hazard model can be written as follows:

$$\lambda\left(t_i \mid x_i\right) = h\left(t; x_i; \beta\right)$$

Three common specifications of duration dependence are when the survivor function is determined by the exponential, Weibull, and log-logistic distribution functions. The simplest specification is when the survivor function is based on the exponential distribution:

$$S(t) = \exp(-\theta\ t)$$

From equation (5.1) above, the corresponding density function is obtained as the derivative of this function with respect to t multiplied by -1:

$$f(t) = \theta \times \exp(-\theta\ t)$$

The hazard rate—obtained by calculating the ratio $\frac{f(t)}{S(t)}$—for the exponential distribution is therefore a constant:

$$\lambda(t) = \theta$$

This is useful as a reference specification and it implies that the mean or expected spell length is $E(t) = \frac{1}{\theta}$. With respect to duration, the survivor function has the usual shape, but the hazard is a horizontal straight line.

A straightforward generalization of this is obtained by raising duration t to the power α in the survivor function:

$$S(t) = \exp(-\theta t^{\alpha})$$

This is the *Weibull* specification, and the hazard function is given by:

$$\lambda(t) = \alpha\ \theta\ t^{\alpha-1} \qquad (5.2)$$

If $\alpha = 1$, the exponential specification is obtained. The hazard function can be increasing with duration $\alpha > 1$ or decreasing $0 < \alpha < 1$, but it will be monotonic (see Fig. 5.4)—it cannot rise and then fall for example.

A more flexible specification, which allows the hazard to increase at first and decline with longer durations, is obtained when the survivor function is given by the *log-logistic* distribution:

$$S(t) = (1 + \theta t^{\alpha})^{-1}$$

The corresponding hazard function is given by:

$$\lambda(t) = \frac{\alpha\theta t^{\alpha-1}}{1 + \theta t^{\alpha}}$$

The hazard rate declines with duration if $\alpha > 1$ and is non-monotonic for values of α between 0 and 1. It is constant when $\alpha = 1$ (see Fig. 5.5).

The parameter α will therefore determine the nature of duration dependence—that is, the way in which the hazard varies with the length of a

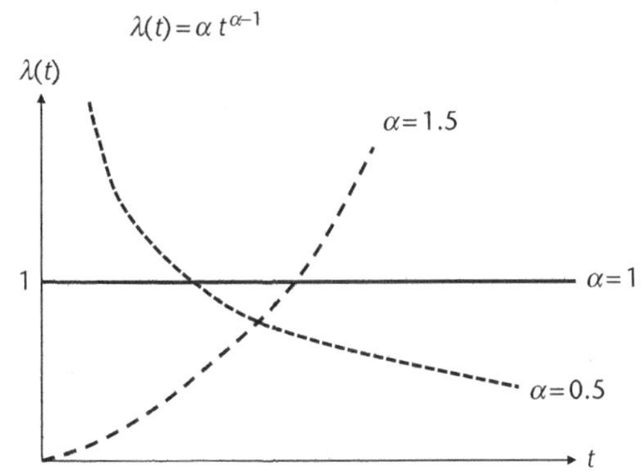

Figure 5.4. Hazard function shapes for the Weibull distribution

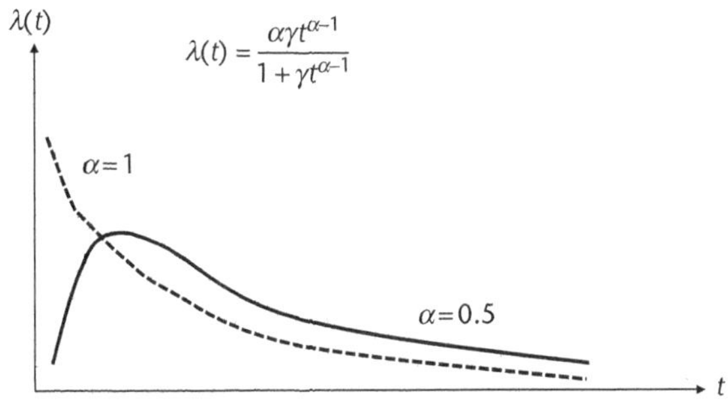

Figure 5.5. Shapes of the hazard function for the log-logistic distribution

spell. The higher the hazard rate, the shorter will be the completed duration. Individual characteristics and labour market conditions will also influence the hazard rate and these are incorporated by specifying θ as a function of these variables:

$$\theta_i = \exp\left(\beta_1 + \beta_2 x_{2i} + \ldots \beta_K x_{Ki}\right) = \exp\left(x_i'\beta\right).$$

Writing this component in this way ensures that the hazard rate is positive. In the case of the exponential and Weibull specifications, the effect of a change in one of the explanatory variables is to shift the hazard curve in a vertical fashion. In the log-logistic case, a variation of an explanatory variable can change the shape of the hazard. If individual characteristics do not affect the hazard, then θ is just a constant ($\theta_i = \exp(\beta_1)$).

Using these specifications of the hazard function constitutes a *parametric* approach. The models are nonlinear in the parameters and, for an assumed distribution of spells, the parameters of interest—the scalar α and the vector

β—can be estimated using maximum likelihood techniques. The likelihood function is defined in terms of the density of the completed spells:

$$L = \prod_{i=1}^{n} f(t_i \mid x_i)$$

From the definition of the hazard function $f(t) = \lambda(t) \times S(t)$ and so, for example, the likelihood function for the Weibull specification is:

$$L = \prod_{i=1}^{n} \alpha\, t_i^{\alpha-1} \times \exp(x_i'\beta) \times \exp\left[-t_i^{\alpha} \exp(x_i'\beta)\right]$$

Data from the 2003 French Labour Force survey on completed durations are used to illustrate the estimation of these parametric hazard models. The sample consists of 2,958 individuals of both sexes. The explanatory variables retained to examine why spells differ in length are age, education, diploma level, marital status, the presence of children, and living in an urban area. The latter can be regarded as the size of the local labour market. Duration dependence is taken into account via the specification of the hazard function. As a benchmark, the exponential distribution for the survivor function is used since there is no duration dependence in this case because the hazard is constant with respect to spell length. The results are presented in Table 5.1.

On the basis of the t statistics, which since the estimates are obtained by maximum likelihood are compared to the 5% critical values of 1.96, there are no differences in the hazard rate between males and females, or individuals with or without children. However being married increases the hazard rate and thus leads to shorter spell lengths. A married person has hazard that is 11% $(=(\exp(0.106) - 1) \times 100\%)$ higher than a single person. A person living in an urban area has lower hazard (by 8.8%) than someone in rural area. For an individual aged 50 the hazard will be 20% lower than for someone aged 40. The key determinant of spell length, however, will be education. Someone with a degree will have a hazard rate which 26% higher $(=(\exp(0.234) - 1) \times 100\%)$ than someone with no diploma, and 8.8% $(=(\exp(0.234 - 0.15) - 1) \times 100\%)$ higher than an identical individual who has only a baccalaureat. The hazard function is thus shifted up and down by differences in the characteristics of the unemployed. When it is shifted downwards, the average spell length will be longer.

Assuming an exponential distribution for the distribution of spell lengths imposes the restriction of no duration dependence. One way of relaxing this constraint is by using a Weibull specification for the survivor function. The additional parameter (α) enables the hypothesis of no duration dependence to be tested. This corresponds to the case where $\alpha = 1$. The results for the hazard model with a Weibull specification are presented in the second

Table 5.1. The determinants of unemployment durations in France—completed durations

Number of observations: 2,958		
Explanatory variables (mean in parentheses)	Exponential model	Weibull hazard model
		$\tilde{\alpha} = 1.12$ (0.016)
Female	−0.011*n* (0.037)	−0.010*n* (0.034)
Married	0.106 (0.045)	0.103 (0.039)
Age	−0.022 (0.002)	−0.022 (0.002)
Secondary diploma	0.088 (0.045)	0.087 (0.040)
Baccalaureat	0.150 (0.059)	0.149 (0.053)
Further education	0.288 (0.069)	0.285 (0.062)
Bachelor/Masters	0.234 (0.067)	0.231 (0.061)
Number of children aged 6 to 18	−0.020*n* (0.022)	−0.019*n* (0.019)
Number of children aged under 6	−0.055*n* (0.036)	−0.053*n* (0.032)
Lives in urban area	−0.092 (0.038)	−0.087 (0.034)
Log likelihood	−4318	−4289

column of Table 5.1. The hypothesis of a constant hazard with respect to spell length is rejected since the absolute value of the test statistic is greater than the critical value of 1.96:

$$\frac{\tilde{\alpha} - 1}{\sqrt{\text{var}(\tilde{\alpha})}} = \frac{1.12 - 1}{0.016} = 7.5$$

This suggests that the hazard rate increases (slowly) with spell length, so that the chances of leaving unemployment improve over time. Apart from the inclusion of positive duration dependence, the effects of the explanatory variables are numerically very close to those of the exponential model.

5.2.3 *The Proportional Hazards Model*

A widely used model for the hazard function is the proportional hazards model. This is where the hazard rate is a product of a duration dependence function—which depends only on time and is referred to as the baseline hazard, $\lambda_B(t)$—and a component that depends only on explanatory variables:

$$\lambda(t_i \mid x_i) = \lambda_B(t) \times \theta(x_i; \beta)$$

The second component is often specified as: $\theta(x_i; \beta) = \exp(x_i'\beta)$. The Weibull specification used above (equation (5.2)) is therefore an example of a proportional hazards model. The parameters of this model can be interpreted in a very straightforward manner. If an explanatory variable, say x_k, increases by one unit the hazard function becomes:

$$\lambda_B(t) \times \exp(x_i'\beta + \beta_k) = \lambda(t_i \mid x_i) \exp(\beta_k)$$

The hazard changes by a factor $\exp(\beta_k)$, and so if $\beta_k > 0$ the hazard rate increases. This is similar to the odds ratio interpretation of coefficients in the logit model (see Chapter 3). Essentially, the baseline hazard function—which is common to all individuals—shifts vertically in a parallel fashion when the explanatory variables change.

The proportional hazards model has the property that *if required* the vector of parameters β can be estimated without specifying the form of the baseline hazard using Cox's (1972) partial likelihood approach, which only contains the terms $\theta(x_i; \beta)$. It is a *semi-parametric* model and it has two advantages over the parametric approach. First, in parametric models, if the form of the hazard (exponential, Wiebull, and so on) is misspecified, the estimates of the parameters (β) will be biased. The Cox approach enables practitioners to avoid this problem. Second, in much of labour economics, the focus is on the effects of characteristics on outcomes and so the parameters of interest are represented by the vector β. The precise form of the hazard is often a secondary consideration.[4] The assumption of a proportional hazard has to be satisfied for these properties to be valid.

5.3 Censoring: Complete and Incomplete Durations

The likelihood functions presented above apply when the spells being analysed are completed durations—that is, the individual has left that state. Most data on unemployment spells will be incomplete durations—the individuals in the sample are still in the state and can provide information concerning when the spell began, but do not know when it will finish. Incomplete duration data alone cannot be used to determine the length of a spell and its determinants except by making specific assumptions about flows into and out of unemployment—see, for example, Nickell (1979). In order to obtain a sample with at least some completed spells, either those recently having found employment are asked retrospective questions about

[4] The survivor function—and therefore the hazard function—however, can be obtained using a non-parametric technique (see, for example, Cameron and Trivedi, 2005, p. 596).

how long they were unemployed prior to obtaining their current job, or a second survey of the same (unemployed) persons is undertaken at some later date. Some of the unemployed will have found work and report a completed duration. Those still unemployed will have incomplete durations and these observations are considered as censored. They are in fact *right-censored* because the starting date of the spell is known but not the exit date.

5.3.1 *The Nonparametric Survivor Function with Incomplete Duration Data*

In the case where some or all of the durations are censored, the most commonly used method to describe durations is the non-parametric one proposed by Kaplan and Meier (1958). As before d_j is the number leaving the state (that is having a completed duration) after a stay of j months. Let c_j be the number of persons who declare an incomplete duration of length j. Define the number of persons remaining unemployed for j months or longer as $m_j = (d_j + c_j) + (d_{j+1} + c_{j+1}) + ... + (d_T + c_T)$. The Kaplan–Meier estimate of survival function at each duration in months is given by:

$$\hat{S}(t) = \left(\frac{m_1 - d_1}{m_1}\right) \times \left(\frac{m_2 - d_2}{m_2}\right) \times \ldots \times \left(\frac{m_t - d_t}{m_t}\right) = \prod_{j=1}^{t} \left(\frac{m_j - d_j}{m_j}\right)$$

$$\text{for} \quad t = 0, 1, \ldots, T$$

Given the implied discrete nature of the data in the definitions of m_j and d_j, an estimate of the corresponding hazard function can be obtained as:

$$\hat{\lambda}(t) = \frac{\text{proportion leaving state in the interval t} + \Delta}{\text{proportion still in state at time t}} = \frac{d_t/n}{m_t/n} = \frac{d_t}{m_t}$$

The survivor function for discrete data can therefore be written in terms of the hazard rate as:

$$\hat{S}(t) = \prod_{j=1}^{t} \left(1 - \frac{d_j}{m_j}\right) = \prod_{j=1}^{t} \left(1 - \hat{\lambda}(j)\right)$$

In order to see how these estimates are obtained, consider the following sample of eight individuals' durations where an asterisk indicates that the observation is censored:

$$1, 1^*, 2, 3, 4, 4^*, 5, 6$$

Table 5.2 presents the different elements of the calculation. Obviously, a sample of eight observations does not provide very reliable estimates, and the resulting graph will resemble that in Fig. 5.2(b). For a large number

Table 5.2. Kaplan–Meier estimate of the survivor function

Duration	m_i	d_i	c_i	$1-\frac{d_i}{m_i}$	$\hat{\lambda}\ (t)$	$\hat{S}\ (t)$
0	8	0	0	$1-\frac{0}{8}=1$	0	1
1	8	1	1	$1-\frac{1}{8}=\frac{7}{8}$	$\frac{1}{8}$	$1\times\frac{7}{8}=\frac{7}{8}$
2	6	1	0	$1-\frac{1}{6}=\frac{5}{6}$	$\frac{1}{6}$	$1\times\frac{7}{8}\times\frac{5}{6}=\frac{35}{48}$
3	5	1	0	$1-\frac{1}{5}=\frac{4}{5}$	$\frac{1}{5}$	$1\times\frac{7}{8}\times\frac{5}{6}\times\frac{4}{5}=\frac{7}{12}$
4	4	1	1	$1-\frac{1}{4}=\frac{3}{4}$	$\frac{1}{4}$	$1\times\frac{7}{8}\times\frac{5}{6}\times\frac{4}{5}\times\frac{3}{4}=\frac{21}{48}$
5	2	1	0	$1-\frac{1}{2}=\frac{1}{2}$	$\frac{1}{2}$	$1\times\frac{7}{8}\times\frac{5}{6}\times\frac{4}{5}\times\frac{1}{2}\times\frac{1}{2}=\frac{7}{32}$
6	1	1	0	0	1	0

of observations, it is useful to smooth these functions using, for example, kernel methods.

5.3.2 *Estimating the Determinants of Completed Durations in the Presence of Censoring*

In the first section of this chapter, it was pointed out that two approaches to modelling the determinants of durations were commonly used. When some of the durations are censored, the hazard specification estimated by maximum likelihood can be extended in a very straightforward and intuitive way to take account of this facet of the data. Accelerated failure time models, which use the observed duration as the left-hand side variable, can also be adapted but this will involve maximum likelihood estimation and so the advantage in terms of facility of estimation is lost.

In order to incorporate censored (that is incomplete) durations in the estimation of hazard models, an additional variable is used. Each observation in the sample consists of a spell length (t_i) and a dummy variable (c_i) which is equal to one for completed spells and zero for incomplete durations. There are thus two types of observation that will be used in the likelihood function.[5]

Completed uncensored durations for which we use: $f(t)=\lambda\,(t)\times S\,(t)$, $c_i=1$.

Incomplete censored durations for which we use: $S(t)$, $c_i=0$.

The likelihood function can therefore be written (which is very similar but not identical to the Tobit likelihood function) as:

$$L=\prod_{c_i=1} f\,(t_i\mid x_i)\prod_{c_i=0} S\,(t_i\mid x_i)$$

[5] These are referred to as 'likelihood contributions'.

This can also be written in terms a single product operator, that is for the whole sample, as:

$$L = \prod_{i=1}^{n} [f(t_i \mid x_i)]^{c_i} \, [S(t_i \mid x_i)]^{1-c_i}$$

Finally, using the definition of the hazard function, the density can be replaced by $f(t) = \lambda(t) \times S(t)$:

$$L = \prod_{i=1}^{n} [\lambda(t_i \mid x_i)]^{c_i} \, [S(t_i \mid x_i)]^{c_i} \, [S(t_i \mid x_i)]^{1-c_i}$$

$$= \prod_{i=1}^{n} [\lambda(t_i \mid x_i)]^{c_i} \, [S(t_i \mid x_i)]$$

The only difference between this and the likelihood when all durations are complete is the power or exponent (c_i) on the hazard term. As pointed out above, for each parametric survivor function it is straightforward to derive the hazard function, and so writing the likelihood function with censored observations is straightforward. For the Weibull specification, the likelihood function is:

$$L = \prod_{i=1}^{n} \left[\alpha t_i^{\alpha-1} \times \exp\left(x_i'\beta\right)\right]^{c_i} \times \exp\left(-t_i^{\alpha} \exp\left(x_i'\beta\right)\right)$$

This model is estimated using data on both complete and incomplete durations from the 2003 French Labour Force survey for the same explanatory variables used in Table 5.1. In addition to the 2,958 completed durations there are 8,817 individuals who were still unemployed by the end of 2003, and so their durations are incomplete and for estimation purposes are right-censored. The estimated Weibull duration dependence parameter is very similar to that obtained with completed durations—see Table 5.3, column 1. Thus there is moderate positive duration dependence according to this model. However, the inclusion of censored durations changes the factors that shift the hazard function up and down. Living in an urban area is found to have no significant influence on the probability of leaving unemployment. The presence of children aged 6 to 18, on the other hand, decreases the hazard rate in a statistically significant manner by an estimated 4.5% compared to childless unemployed persons. Those with more education will have shorter spell lengths.

The weakness of the Weibull specification is that the hazard rate either rises with spell length or it declines over the whole spell length. This specification does not permit the hazard to take a non-monotonic form—rise initially and then decrease as the spell becomes very long. The latter phenomenon

Table 5.3. The determinants of unemployment durations in France—complete and incomplete durations

Number of observations: 11,675; censored 8,817			
Explanatory variables (mean in parentheses)	Weibull hazard model	Log-logistic hazard model	Proportional hazards model
Duration dependence	$\tilde{\alpha} = 1.13$ (0.016)	$\tilde{\alpha} = 0.78$ (0.011)	– –
Female	−0.022*n* (0.033)	−0.025*n* (0.036)	−0.031*n* (0.037)
Married	0.105 (0.039)	0.119 (0.043)	0.112 (0.044)
Age	−0.019 (0.002)	−0.021 (0.002)	−0.019 (0.003)
Secondary diploma	0.096 (0.040)	0.100 (0.044)	0.107 (0.045)
Baccalaureat	0.138 (0.053)	0.137 (0.064)	0.139 (0.059)
Further education	0.280 (0.062)	0.298 (0.068)	0.297 (0.070)
Bachelor/Masters	0.243 (0.060)	0.262 (0.066)	0.257 (0.068)
Number of children aged 6 to 18	−0.044 (0.019)	−0.047 (0.020)	−0.050 (0.021)
Number of children aged under 6	−0.014*n* (0.032)	−0.025*n* (0.034)	−0.012*n* (0.036)
Live in urban area	−0.059*n* (0.034)	−0.083 (0.037)	−0.061*n* (0.038)
Log likelihood	−8.297	−8.313	Partial likelihood used

might be appropriate though in countries where the proportion of long term unemployed is persistently high. For this group, the hazard rate must be very low. One parametric specification that permits this form of duration dependence is the log-logistic distribution. The estimated parameter shape is $\tilde{\alpha} = 0.78$, and since it lies between zero and one, the hazard is indeed increasing then decreasing—see Fig. 5.5. Other than this, the effects of the explanatory variables are the same as for the Weibull model. One final check can be undertaken by factoring out duration dependence using the proportional hazards specification. This confirms that the effects of the explanatory variables are not dependent on the parametric specification chosen for the hazard. Married persons, highly educated individuals, and the relatively young will have shorter completed durations of unemployment. Those with children, persons not in a couple, individuals with a low education level, and older persons will generally have longer spells of unemployment.

5.4 Modelling Issues with Duration Data

It is clear from the methods presented in this chapter that the econometric analysis of duration data is more complicated than for other forms of data. The underlying concepts are different from regression models and there are a number of key decisions that have to be made by the practitioner before a model can be estimated. In this final section, we examine three important issues that arise when modelling with duration data. The first concerns unobserved heterogeneity. This has already been examined in earlier chapters in the context of the linear regression model, and was found to introduce bias if unobserved factors were correlated with the included explanatory variables. Second, the models treated above were based on parametric specifications, and in line with the general approach adopted in this book, where possible it is advisable to test whether the assumptions made are valid or not. We outline one method that can be used with duration data. Finally, the discrete nature of much duration data means that the smooth parametric functional forms used for the survivor and hazard functions may not be appropriate. In particular, the way in which duration dependence is modelled needs special attention.

5.4.1 *Unobserved Heterogeneity*

As with other econometric approaches, hazard models are specified by the practitioner. Errors of specification can occur at different points in the exercise and concern the form of duration dependence, the functional form linking the explanatory variables to the hazard, and the omission of relevant explanatory variables. Sometimes these are variables that are not present in the data set or simply individual characteristics that are inherently unobservable, such as an individual's drive or work ethic. Practitioners have been particularly concerned by unobserved (or excluded) heterogeneity since it can lead to substantial bias in the estimated parameters of interest. The prominent concern is that individuals may differ in their chances of leaving unemployment as a result of these unobserved characteristics. Those with favourable characteristics will leave unemployment quickly, and so the sample of observed durations will contain more longer durations than a randomly chosen sample. This can lead to the estimated hazard at a given duration for a given set of observed characteristics being lower than is in fact the case, thus understating the degree of duration dependence. For example, for the Weibull hazard specification:

$$\lambda(t_i \mid x_i) = \alpha\, t^{\alpha-1} \exp\left(x_i'\beta\right)$$

unobserved heterogeneity leads to underestimation of α and β is biased towards zero (from the positive or negative side). The proportionality of the hazard can also be invalidated.

A commonly used means of incorporating unobserved heterogeneity is to treat it as a random variable (v_i) which enters the hazard in a multiplicative fashion:

$$\lambda(t_i \mid x_i , v_i) = \alpha\, t^{\alpha-1} \exp\left(x_i'\beta\right) \times v_i$$

This unobservable factor is often assumed to follow a Gamma distribution, with mean equal to one (this is a normalization) and variance equal to $\mathrm{var}\,(v_i) = \frac{1}{\delta}$. This adds a term to the likelihood function and there is an additional parameter to be estimated. As with linear regression, if the source of the bias is included in the estimation process, the resulting estimates are not subject to bias.

5.4.2 *Evaluating the Appropriateness of the Parametric Specification*

Research into specification testing in econometrics is an ongoing activity. Analysing relations between variables, however, requires the practitioner to propose a model and an appropriate estimation technique. In hazard models, as we have seen, an assumption is required for the distribution of completed durations and this will determine not only the hazard function but also the survivor function. As has been stressed throughout this book, where possible, it is a good idea to test the adequacy of any strong assumptions that are made. One of the more common approaches is to use (estimated) residual plots and compare them to what they should be if the parametric assumption is correct.

The links between the different representations of durations—hazard, density, survivor, and integrated hazard—are always valid in theory. However, they may not be when estimated parameters are used in place of the unknown population parameters. The residual used with hazard models is called the *generalized residual*[6] and is given by the estimate of integrated hazard defined as:

$$\varepsilon\left(T^*\right) = \int_0^{T^*} \tilde{\lambda}(t)\, dt$$

If the specification used for the hazard is compatible with the properties of the data, this generalized residual should be equal to $-\log S\left(\int_0^{T^*} \tilde{\lambda}\,(t)\, dt\right)$ where $S(.)$ is the survivor function corresponding to the assumed form of the hazard function and $\tilde{\lambda}$ is the estimated value of the hazard function.

[6] This is also referred to as the 'Cox–Snell' residual.

For example, if the Weibull specification is used for the hazard function, the integrated hazard function is $\Lambda(t) = t^{\alpha} \exp(x_i'\beta)$—see the Appendix to this chapter. The generalized residual is calculated using the estimated values of α and β:

$$\varepsilon(t) = t^{\tilde{\alpha}} \exp\left(x_i'\tilde{\beta}\right)$$

If the Weibull specification is the appropriate one then, for each duration, this generalized residual should be approximately equal to $-\log S(\varepsilon(t))$ where $S(\varepsilon(t))$ is calculated as the proportion of individuals for which the generalized residual is greater than $\varepsilon(t)$. By plotting the generalized residual against the latter, the scatter plot should be close to the 45° line.

5.4.3 *Discrete Duration Data*

In the first sections of this chapter, the methods presented apply to durations in continuous time whereas in practice most observations will apply to intervals such as weeks and months. This is referred to as *grouped data.*[7] Thus, instead of the smooth survivor and hazard functions described by the parametric forms considered above, step functions will apply. This has already been seen using the Kaplan–Meier method. Discrete data also modifies the definitions of the hazard and survivor functions, and can make estimating duration models more straightforward. First, the numerator of the hazard function is the density defined at a given duration. Given that the unit of observation here is an interval, the numerator is the difference between two values of the survivor function. The hazard with discrete data can therefore be interpreted as the probability that an individual ends a spell of unemployment in the jth week, defined by the interval a_{j-1}, a_j, and is expressed as:

$$\lambda(a_j) = \frac{\text{Prob}\left(a_{j-1} < T \leq a_j\right)}{\text{Prob}\left(T > a_{j-1}\right)} = \frac{S\left(a_{j-1}\right) - S\left(a_j\right)}{S\left(a_{j-1}\right)} = 1 - \frac{S\left(a_j\right)}{S\left(a_{j-1}\right)}$$

Second, the probability of remaining unemployed or 'surviving' up to week m defined by the interval a_{m-1}, a_m, is the following product:

$$S(a_m) = (1 - \lambda(a_1)) \times (1 - \lambda(a_2)) \times \ldots (1 - \lambda(a_{m-1})) \times (1 - \lambda(a_m))$$

$$= \prod_{j=1}^{m} (1 - \lambda(a_j)) \qquad (5.3)$$

[7] Although of this type of data is treated as discrete, the spell lengths are not *intrinsically discrete*. The information available is that a spell is observed or ends on a given day or in a given week or month. Intrinsically discrete data are when the spell can only end on a Friday for example.

This will be the likelihood contribution for someone with an incomplete (censored) duration at week m.

An individual who leaves unemployment in the interval a_{m-1}, a_m will have survived through the periods up to a_{m-1}, and so the density at date a_m in the discrete case is written as:

$$f(a_m) = \lambda(a_m) \times S(a_{m-1})$$

From the definition of the survivor function, $S(a_m) = \prod_{j=1}^{m} (1 - \lambda(a_j))$, the following equality can be used:

$$S(a_{m-1}) = \frac{S(a_m)}{1 - \lambda(a_m)}$$

$$\text{so that} \quad f(a_m) = \frac{\lambda(a_m)}{1 - \lambda(a_m)} \times S(a_m) \tag{5.4}$$

Recalling that the likelihood function for right-censored data is given by:

$$L = \prod_{i=1}^{n} [f(t_i \mid x_i)]^{c_i} [S(t_i \mid x_i)]^{1-c_i}$$

where $c_i = 1$ for completed durations, the values of the density and survivor functions defined by equations (5.2) and (5.4) are substituted in.

As pointed out by Allison (1984) and Jenkins (1995), the corresponding *log likelihood* function can be expressed in a form that can be estimated using a simple logit model (see the Appendix to this chapter for details). By defining the dummy variable $\delta_{im} = 1$ for the week in which individual i's spell ends and $\delta_{ij} = 0$ for all the preceding weeks of the spell, and $\delta_{ij} = 0$ for every week (including $j = m$) of an incomplete spell, the log likelihood takes the same form as that for a binary dependent variable (such as the logit):

$$\log L = \sum_{i=1}^{n} \sum_{j=1}^{m} [\delta_{ij} \log(\lambda(a_{ji})) + (1 - \delta_{ij}) \log(1 - \lambda(a_{ji}))]$$

This easy route to estimating a duration model with censoring is made possible by setting up the data in a particular way by a process of *episode-splitting*. For each individual, who has a duration of $t_i = m$ weeks, m records are created (in place of just one)—one for each week of the spell. The data will be in person-weeks (this is the meaning of the double sum in the log likelihood function). Naturally, the hazard function specification to be estimated using this approach should include the individual's characteristics as well as a variable representing the length of the spell in order to capture any duration dependence. Using the logistic specification for $\lambda(a_{ji})$, the parameters of the hazard function can be obtained by estimating a logit model for Prob $(\delta_{ij} = 1)$ on this data set:

$$\text{Prob}\left(\delta_{ij} = 1\right) = \frac{1}{1 + \exp\left(-\lambda_0(t) - x_i'\beta\right)}$$

This approach to estimating duration models turns out to be very useful. First, the parameters of interest can be estimated using standard econometric routines (the logit procedure) and can be adapted to incorporate other features of the data on durations such as truncated spells. Second, it is straightforward to incorporate time-varying explanatory variables. If we only had one observation per individual in the likelihood function, how would we deal with a variable that changed during an individual's spell of unemployment? For example, eligibility for unemployment and related benefits changes with the length of a spell of unemployment and is therefore time-varying. Other relevant variables of this type would be periods of training undertaken while unemployed, deterioration of health status, and changes in family circumstances.

5.5 Concluding Remarks

The literature on modelling durations is vast and in this chapter the key elements relevant to empirical labour economics have been presented. The presentation has been in terms of unemployment durations as this represents the most common application of these techniques in labour economics. However the same tools can be used to analyse the determinants of the length of a spell in any kind of state—maternity leave, benefit receipt, sick leave, a period spent in training, or the length of a job (or job tenure).

The tools have been illustrated using limited, but commonly used, types of duration dependence and the models have been based on parametric specifications. Naturally many variations and extensions of these approaches are used in practice. First, the nature of data available will mean that the tools presented here will have to be adapted to take into account any particularities. Second, the approaches presented here refer to a single spell in a given state with transition out of that state. In practice, over a given period, individuals may return to that same state—for example, after a temporary job or finding and losing a job in a short space of time. This is called multiple cycle analysis. Third, we might be interested in the state to which an individual moves after unemployment (part-time employment, self-employment, outside the labour force, and so on). This can be analysed using a competing risks model. Finally, it should be emphasized that the role and treatment of unobserved heterogeneity is a key area of ongoing research.

Further Reading

An excellent reference is Keifer's (1988) survey article which provides an account of duration models for the applied economist. Jenkins (2005) has a very clear and thorough presentation on survival analysis for practitioners, especially those who use STATA. Allison's (1995) book for users of SAS is also very accessible. On the problems related to the form in which the data are observed, the key reference is Salant (1977). An important study that has influenced empirical practice is Meyer's (1990) article. The classic, though fairly advanced, reference on the econometric analysis of duration data is Lancaster's (1992) book. A more recent advanced treatment can be found in Cameron and Trivedi (2005).

Appendix

1. The expected duration of completed spell is equal to the integral of the survival function

The expected value of a (non-negative) random variable over its whole support $[0, T]$ is defined as

$$E(t) = \int_0^T tf(t)\ dt$$

Integrating by parts yields:

$$E(t) = T - \int_0^T F(t)\ dt$$

The integral of the survivor function is equal to right-hand side of this expression. From the definition of the survivor function

$$S(t) = \text{Prob}\left(d > t\right) = 1 - \text{F}(t)$$

The integral can be written as:

$$\int_0^T S(t)\ dt = \int_0^T (1 - \text{F}(t))\ dt$$

$$= [t]_0^T - \int_0^T \text{F}(t)\ dt = T - \int_0^T \text{F}(t)\ dt = E(t)$$

2. The integrated hazard function

Using the definition of the density and survivor functions:

$$f(t) = \frac{\partial F(t)}{\partial t} = -\frac{\partial S(t)}{\partial t}$$

the hazard function can be expressed as

$$\lambda(t) = -\frac{\frac{\partial S(t)}{\partial t}}{S(t)} = -\frac{\partial \log S(t)}{\partial t}$$

The integral of the hazard rate up to a given duration, say T^*, is then:

$$\Lambda(T^*) = \int_0^{T^*} \lambda(t)\,dt = -\int_0^{T^*} \frac{\partial \log S(t)}{\partial t} dt$$

$$= -\log S(T^*) + \log S(0) = -\log S(T^*)$$

since $S(0) = 1$ so that $\log S(0) = 0$. Thus the survivor function can be obtained as:

$$S(T^*) = \exp\left(-\int_0^{T^*} \lambda(t)\,dt\right)$$

The integrated hazard plays a useful role in linking the various means of representing duration data since it links the hazard function (which is often the function that is estimated) back to the survivor function, and ultimately to the expected or mean duration. For the Weibull hazard function, the value of the integrated hazard up to a duration of T^* is:

$$\Lambda(T^*) = \int_0^{T^*} \exp(x_i'\beta)\ \alpha t^{\alpha-1} dt = \exp(x_i'\beta) \int_0^{T^*} \alpha t^{\alpha-1} dt = T^{*\alpha} \exp(x_i'\beta)$$

3. The log likelihood function with discrete (grouped) duration data

Recalling that the likelihood function for right-censored data is given by:

$$L = \prod_{i=1}^{n} [f(t_i \mid x_i)]^{c_i} [S(t_i \mid x_i)]^{1-c_i}$$

where $c_i = 1$ for completed durations, the likelihood function for discrete data will be:

$$L = \prod_{i=1}^{n} \left[\frac{\lambda(a_j)}{1-\lambda(a_j)} \times S(a_j)\right]^{c_i} [S(a_j)]^{1-c_i}$$

Substituting in from the definition of the survivor function, the likelihood function is now:

$$L = \prod_{i=1}^{n} \left[\left(\frac{\lambda(a_{mi})}{1-\lambda(a_{mi})}\right)^{c_i} \prod_{j=1}^{m} 1-\lambda(a_{ji})\right]$$

For each individual, the value of the hazard for each week from the beginning of his/her entry into unemployment to the time of exit (for completed spells) or censoring (for incomplete durations) is used in the definition of the likelihood function. The logarithm of this function that is to be maximized is:

$$\log L = \sum_{i=1}^{n} c_i \log\left(\frac{\lambda\left(a_{mi}\right)}{1-\lambda\left(a_{mi}\right)}\right) + \sum_{i=1}^{n}\sum_{j=1}^{m} \log\left(1-\lambda\left(a_{ji}\right)\right)$$

By defining the dummy variable $\delta_{im} = 1$ for the week in which individual i's spell ends and $\delta_{ij} = 0$ for all the preceding weeks of the spell, and $\delta_{ij} = 0$ for every week (including $j = m$) of an incomplete spell, the log likelihood function can be written in the following way:

$$\log L = \sum_{i=1}^{n}\sum_{j=1}^{m} \left[\delta_{ij} \log\left(\lambda\left(a_{ji}\right)\right) + \left(1-\delta_{ij}\right)\log\left(1-\lambda\left(a_{ji}\right)\right)\right]$$

6

Evaluation of Policy Measures

Since the early 1990s, empirical analysis in labour economics has been increasingly based on establishing causal relations between variables using techniques initially developed for policy evaluation. Instead of obtaining a specific relationship from theoretical reasoning and estimating a structural model or a fairly loose but theoretically inspired reduced form, empirical practice has concentrated on emulating the experimental approach. Although real-life experiments have become more common as this approach has gained ground, they have traditionally been rare in labour economics. The US negative income tax experiments of the 1970s represent some of the first uses.

One of the first arguments made for emulating an experimental approach can be found in Lalonde's (1986) critique of econometric modelling of the effect of training programmes. Using experimental data, he was able to compare the outcome obtained by comparing two groups, one of which was randomly selected to receive training. Compared to the control group—those not selected for training—annual earnings of those participating in the programme were found, on average, to be more than $800 higher. Given random assignment to the programme, these experimental estimates can be regarded as reliable. An econometric approach using a selectivity model produces divergent results, and is unable to reproduce anything like the experimental estimates. Card and Krueger's (1995) famous study of the 1992 New Jersey minimum wage hike, with its striking conclusions, reinforced the usefulness of this approach. The recent textbook by Angrist and Pischke (2009), written from an explicitly quasi-experimental standpoint, is an indication of the extent to which empirical analysis in labour economics has assimilated this approach.

One of the main advantages of working with experimental data is that the estimates obtained are model-free, in the sense that they do not depend on a structural model of behaviour or specific distributional assumptions.

This, of course, requires that the sample used really is generated by an experiment in which there is random assignment of individuals into 'treated' and 'control' groups. Interfering in people's lives, by reducing their incomes or discriminating in favour of certain persons for training, employment, or financial aid, is a highly sensitive issue and raises many ethical questions. As such, experiments with random assignment tend to be rare in labour economics. However, there are situations which come about in a very similar manner to running a randomized experiment. For example, in the US, when one state changes a law or introduces a progamme and neighbouring states do not, this creates a 'natural experiment'. Apart from their address, there is good reason to believe that the populations in the same geographical region have similar characteristics. Teenagers in one county have very similar characteristics to teenagers in the neighbouring county, for example. The use of pilot studies in particular geographical areas also produces natural experimental data. Policies that apply to persons on the basis of some observable personal characteristic (such as age) provide a similar basis for policy evaluation, since a control group is defined on the basis of observed characteristics and selection into the programme is not endogenous (in the sense of eligibility).

However, a large part of empirical analysis in labour economics continues to be based on non-experimental (that is, survey) data including studies seeking to estimate the impact of a programme or policy measure. Applying an experimental approach to estimating this impact will generally be made difficult on the one hand by self-selection mechanisms and on the other by the absence of a well-defined control group. In this chapter, we will present different methods of undertaking policy evaluation using these kinds of situations. The basic framework for analysing pure experimental data is first set out, since this provides the key to the popularity of such an approach. We will also see how the experimental estimates obtained can be viewed as regression estimates, that is comparing the mean outcomes for the treated group and the control group. This provides a link with material presented in earlier chapters as well as a means of adapting econometric tools in order undertake policy evaluation.

6.1 The Experimental Approach

The effect or impact of a measure is the difference between (a) what is observed in the presence of the measure and (b) what would have occurred in its absence. For a given individual, i, the effect of a measure on an outcome variable, say y_i, is defined as the difference between what is observed in the presence of the measure (y_i^1) and the value of that variable (y_i^0) that would have prevailed in the absence of the measure. Since for each individual we can only observe one of these, a direct estimate of the effect of the measure for an individual is not possible.

However, it is possible in certain circumstances to estimate the impact of a measure in terms of its effect on the *mean* of an outcome variable (employment, earnings, unemployment duration, and so on). This is called the *average treatment effect.*[1] While we do not observe the mean of the variable in the absence of the measure for those affected, in an experiment where two groups from the same population are randomly assigned into a treated group (1) and a control group (0), the mean of the variable y in the control group will be equal to the mean for the treated group that would have prevailed in the absence of the measure.

Given that so many articles adopt the same presentation, it is worth spelling this out further.[2] Assignment to the treated group is represented by the dummy variable $d_i = 1$. For a given individual, the value of y_i in the presence of the measure is y_i^1; for the same individual, in the absence of the measure we would observe y_i^0. The average treatment effect is then:

$$\Delta = E\left(y_i^1 - y_i^0 \mid d_i = 1\right)$$

Because the expectation operator applies additively, that is $E(A+B) = E(A) + E(B)$, the effect can also be written as:

$$\Delta = E\left(y_i^1 \mid d_i = 1\right) - E\left(y_i^0 \mid d_i = 1\right)$$

Obviously the second term is never observed—individuals 'receive treatment' ($d_i = 1$) and so cannot have an observable value of y_i^0. However, in an experimental approach with random assignment into treated and control groups, the control group is a random sample drawn from the same population as those treated, but does not benefit from the measure. In parallel to the treated group, we can define for each individual in the control group the two values of y: that which is observed, y_i^0, and the value that would have been observed if the individual had benefited from the measure y_i^1. Obviously the second of these cannot be observed—members of this group are not selected for treatment—but the first can be observed and the average value of y_i^0 in the control group is: $E\left(y_i^0 \mid d_i = 0\right)$.

Taking the average treatment effect as defined above, and adding and subtracting $E\left(y_i^0 \mid d_i = 0\right)$, we have:

[1] Strictly speaking this is the 'average treatment effect on the treated'. An alternative measure is the effect of the programme on a randomly selected individual.

[2] Wooldridge (2002) provides a very clear and comprehensive treatment of the technicalities underlying this framework.

$$\Delta = E\left(y_i^1 \mid d_i = 1\right) - E\left(y_i^0 \mid d_i = 0\right) \quad + \quad E\left(y_i^0 \mid d_i = 0\right) - E\left(y_i^0 \mid d_i = 1\right)$$

Since randomization, by definition, means that $E(y_i^0 | d_i = 0) = E(y_i^0 | d_i = 1)$, the last two terms cancel out. That is what would have happened *on average* in the absence of the measure for those treated is exactly the same as what actually happens on average to those in the control group, since both groups are drawn randomly from the same population.

Randomization means that the average effect of the measure (the average treatment effect) can be calculated as the difference between two means:

$$\Delta = E\left(y_i^1 \mid d_i = 1\right) - E\left(y_i^0 \mid d_i = 0\right)$$

For a sample of $n_0 + n_1 = n$ individuals, where $d_i = 1$ for n_1 individuals, this difference can be calculated as:

$$\hat{\Delta} = \bar{y}^1 - \bar{y}^0$$

where $\bar{y}^j = \frac{1}{n_j} \sum_{i=1}^{n_j} y_i^j$ is the mean value of y_i for each group $j = 0,\ 1$.

A very useful fact in this context is that the same numerical estimate is obtained by estimating β in the following regression using OLS:

$$y_i = \alpha + \beta\, d_i + u_i \quad \text{where} \quad \hat{\beta} = \bar{y}^1 - \bar{y}^0$$

(see the Appendix for details).

It is important to remember that the above derivation is in terms of *averages*. The justification of the estimator of the average treatment effect is contingent on there being random assignment to treated and control groups. However, in a labour economics context, it is rare for an assignment to be undertaken on a random basis, even though we are now seeing more experiments with this feature—no doubt because of the increased demand for this type of data by empirical analysts and policy-makers. In practice, most policy evaluation is undertaken using non-experimental observational data (such as survey data). In certain cases, it is possible to emulate the experimental approach and in particular the link between the average treatment effect and the parameters of a linear regression can be exploited when using non-experimental data.

6.2 The Quasi-experimental Approach—A Control Group can be Defined Exogenously

In the case of 'natural experiments', where a policy is introduced for a particular geographical area or where a measure applies to or is extended to (or withdrawn from) a specific demographic group, empirical analysis can be undertaken in a similar way to the experimental approach because there are fairly well-defined treated and control groups, and the policy is applied in an *exogenous* fashion. Thus, for treated and control groups with identical characteristics, the average treatment effect can be calculated as above.

However, it is not always possible to proceed 'as if' there were random assignment to the two groups. In a geographically defined natural experiment, where treated and control groups come from contiguous geographical areas, there is no guarantee that the two underlying populations will have the same characteristics. This is where the regression equivalence for estimating the average treatment effect is helpful. Since the parameter of interest is the coefficient on the treatment dummy (β) and there is concern that differences in characteristics may be correlated with this dummy, the inclusion of a vector of explanatory variables (x_i) in the estimating equation enables these observable differences to be taken into account:

$$y_i = \alpha + \beta\, d_i + \theta' x_i + u_i$$

Unbiased estimation of β hinges on there being no correlation between the treatment dummy (d_i) and the unobserved factors (u_i) that influence the outcome variable (y_i). This requires that the following condition holds:

$$E\left(u_i \mid x_i,\ d_i\right) = 0$$

This is called the *conditional mean independence* condition,[3] and is satisfied if conditional on observed characteristics, x_i, there is no self-selection into the treated group (or for that matter into the control group). Random assignment automatically guarantees that this condition is met. However, when non-experimental data are used, this assumption may not be satisfied and we return to this in later sections.

If data are available on the two groups *prior* to the policy change, that is we have panel data, then time-invariant non-observable differences between the two groups can also be taken into account and their influence on the estimated treatment effect neutralized. This involves calculating the variation over time in the outcome variable (y_i)—the before-after difference—for each of the groups. The difference in the variation of y_i for each group is the average treatment effect and is known as the *differences-in-differences* (DID) estimator. It is calculated as follows:

(a) Calculate the mean of the outcome variable prior to the implementation of the measure for each of the groups: $\bar{y}_1^B$ and $\bar{y}_0^B$ for the treated and control groups (1 and 0, respectively) where 'B' stands for 'before'.

[3] This is one particular feature of the more general concept of conditional independence which is the usual the assumption made, and which obviously concerns other aspects of the conditional distribution of the error term than the mean.

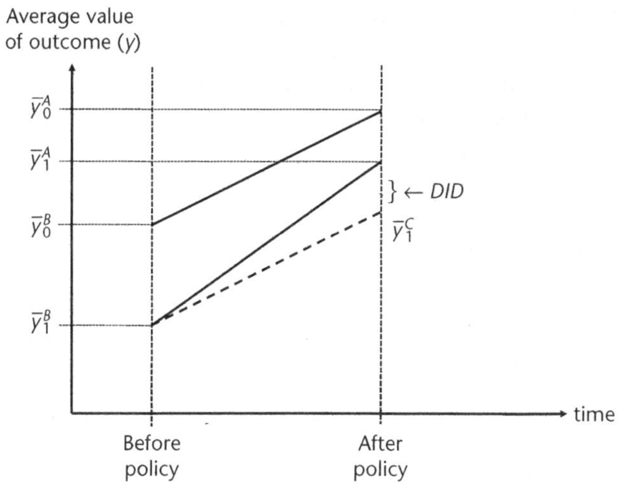

Figure 6.1. The differences-in-differences estimate of a policy measure

In the case of random assignment to treatment, these would be the same because the two groups are drawn randomly from the same population.

(b) Calculate the mean of the outcome variable after the implementation of the measure for each of the groups: $\bar{y}_1^A$ and $\bar{y}_0^A$ where 'A' stands for 'after'.

The DID estimate of the effect of the measure on the treated group is:

$$\hat{\Delta}_D = (\bar{y}_1^A - \bar{y}_1^B) - (\bar{y}_0^A - \bar{y}_0^B)$$

Intuitively, this assumes that the evolution of the average value of y_i for the treated group would have been the same as for the control group in the absence of the measure. This is illustrated in Fig. 6.1. Thus while for the treated group the mean of the outcome variable rises from $\bar{y}_1^B$ to $\bar{y}_1^A$, in the absence of the policy measure it would have increased anyway in line with change in $\bar{y}_0$. The counter-factual mean of the outcome is calculated on the basis of the increase in $\bar{y}_0$ and is equal to $\bar{y}_1^C$. The differences-in-differences estimate of the effect of the policy is therefore $\bar{y}_1^A - \bar{y}_1^C$ which is numerically identical to $\hat{\Delta}_D = (\bar{y}_1^A - \bar{y}_1^B) - (\bar{y}_0^A - \bar{y}_0^B)$. The difference between the DID estimate and the average treatment effect mentioned above is that the time dimension is taken into account, in the sense that the value of the outcome variable y in the absence of treatment can vary over time. The important requirement for obtaining reliable estimates of the treatment effect is that y would evolve in exactly the same manner for the two groups in the absence of the treatment.

As with the average treatment effect above, the same numerical value of the DID estimator can be obtained from a least squares regression by using y_{it} for $t = B$, A and the dummy variable $T_t = 1$ for the period A (after the introduction of the measure). The differences-in-differences estimator is the OLS estimator of β in the following regression[4] using the $2 \times n$ sample observations:

$$y_{it} = \alpha + \beta \left(T_t \times d_i\right) + \delta_1 d_i + \delta_2 T_t + u_{it}$$

This method of estimating the average treatment effect is more likely (than an 'after only' analysis) to satisfy conditional mean independence, since any time-invariant unobserved component that may be correlated with the treatment dummy will be 'differenced out'.

6.2.1 *Minimum Wages and Employment*

One of most well-known studies in modern labour economics involving a natural experiment is Card and Krueger's (1994) analysis of an increase in the minimum wage in the state of New Jersey. In April 1992 the latter rose from \$4.25 (the going federal rate which had been set in June 1991) to \$5.05—an increase of nearly 19%. Prior to the new rate becoming applicable, they undertook a survey of fast food restaurants in New Jersey and in the part of the neighbouring state of Pennsylvania that was close to the New Jersey state line. A large proportion of workers in such establishments are employed on low wages, so that in New Jersey the sample constitutes a 'treated' group. In 1992, Pennsylvania did not change its minimum wage nor did the federal government, and so the Pennsylvania sample constitutes a 'control' group. The same establishments were surveyed some six months after the New Jersey policy change. Given the similarity of the two groups and the clear distinction between treated and non-treated, Card and Krueger were able to use a quasi-experimental basis for assessing the impact of the rise in the minimum wage. Their principal result is presented in Table 6.1. Average employment per restaurant rose very slightly in New Jersey. However, on the basis of the hypothesis that in the absence of the minimum wage increase employment would have evolved in the same manner as in the control group, employment in New Jersey without the minimum wage hike would have *decreased* by about two full-time workers per restaurant. Thus, *because*

[4] An alternative DID estimate can be obtained with explanatory variables in the following regression: $y_{it} = \alpha + \beta \left(T_t \times d_i\right) + \delta_1 d_i + \delta_2 T_t + \theta' x_{it} + u_{it}$.

Table 6.1. Card and Krueger's difference-in-differences estimates of the New Jersey 1992 minimum wage hike

Average employment per restaurant	February 1992	November 1992	Change
New Jersey	29.8	30.0	+0.2
Pennsylvania	33.1	30.9	-2.2
Differences-in-differences			+2.4

Source: Card and Krueger (1994)

of the minimum wage increase, employment increased in New Jersey by 2.4 workers per restaurant—two full-time and one part-time.

This result is quite powerful. It is not based on the specification of a structural econometric model. The counter-factual situation is well-defined and comparable, and the outcome is clearly at odds with the competitive view of the working of the labour market: an exogenous increase in price should lead to a reduction in quantity demanded. Not surprisingly, Card and Krueger's study has been criticized, re-examined, replicated, and given rise to a good deal of debate (see Bazen and Le Gallo (2009) and Neumark and Wascher's (2006) survey).

6.2.2 *Labour Supply and Incentives*

Another major area in labour economics concerns policy measures that are aimed at providing incentives for individuals to change their labour force status, for example, reducing dependence on welfare benefits for the long term unemployed or single parents. In these situations, the outcome variable is usually a dummy variable. The methods presented hitherto in this section apply equally to this case and the average treatment effect refers to the impact of being treated on the participation rate. An interesting natural experiment in this context occurred in 1994 in France with the extension of the payment of a benefit to mothers with young children who remain outside of the labour force. This measure, called the Allocation Parentale d'Education or APE, involves a payment of slightly more than 60 times the gross value of the hourly minimum wage to a mother with children and at least one child aged under 3. It makes part-time work particularly unattractive for the persons concerned. Prior to 1994, this measure applied to mothers with three children or more, but a reform introduced in that year extended it to mothers with two children. For evaluation purposes, this situation can be regarded as a 'natural experiment' and the effect on female labour force participation has been studied in this vein by Piketty (1998). The treated group are then mothers with two children (one of whom is under three), and the control group can be women either with one child or those with more than two children. Both groups can provide a counter-factual situation. A simple differences-in-differences analysis using the first group as the control suggests that the participation of mothers of two children decreased substantially in the three years following the reform (see Table 6.2). The participation rate of mothers of two children is generally lower than that for those with one child, but it fell substantially both numerically and relative to that of mothers of one child. The differences-in-differences estimate of the effect on the participation rate is -13 percentage points.

However, in this case it is not clear that the chosen control group is fully comparable with the females who can benefit from the reform and so it is appropriate to use the equivalence between estimated treatment effects and estimated regression parameters in the equation above. The relevant outcome variable in this is labour force participation and so the dependent variable is a dummy variable. When modelling the probability of an event conditional on a set of explanatory variables, practitioners generally use a logit or probit model. These nonlinear models have the advantage of producing estimated probabilities which lie inside the zero-one interval. If being treated is also represented by a dummy variable, then there is no numerical equivalence between the average treatment effect and the estimated coefficient (as in a linear regression as in the cases above). In this case, the marginal effect for the dummy variable has to be calculated.

The logit and probit models are both constructed using a stochastic underlying latent relation:

$$y_i^* = \alpha + \beta\, d_i + \theta\,' x_i + u_i \text{ where } y_i^* > 0 \Rightarrow y_i = 1$$

The error term is assumed to be distributed according to the normal (probit) or logistic (logit) distribution. As with the marginal effect of a dummy variable in these models, in the case where there is no correlation between excluded unobserved factors and being treated, the effect of being treated is

Table 6.2. Piketty's difference-in-differences estimates of the effect of benefits on female participation in France

Participation rate in	March 1994	March 1997	Change (percentage points)
Mothers with one child under 3	62.0	64.5	+2.5
Mothers with two children (of whom one is under 3)	58.6	47.4	-11.2
Differences-in-differences			-13.7

Source: Piketty (1998)

given by:

$$\Delta = \text{Prob}\left(y_i = 1 \mid x_i,\ d_i = 1\right) - \text{Prob}\left(y_i = 1 \mid x_i,\ d_i = 0\right)$$

Estimation of the parameters by maximum likelihood enables this treatment effect to be estimated as:

$$\tilde{\Delta} = \mathrm{F}\left(\tilde{\alpha} + \tilde{\beta} + \tilde{\theta}'\bar{x}\right) - \mathrm{F}\left(\tilde{\alpha} + \tilde{\theta}'\bar{x}\right)$$

The marginal effect is evaluated for an individual with average characteristics, $\bar{x}$. Since these functions are nonlinear, there is no simple parametric interpretation as in the case of linear regression. Piketty (1998) in fact uses a probit model in order to control for differences in observable characteristics and to make the counter-factual as comparable as possible. Among the explanatory variables included in the x_i vector are education, age, number of children, marital status, and place of residence. The estimated average treatment effect obtained is around −17 percentage points. This confirms the direction of the impact of the measure (non-market time is a normal good) but more importantly indicates that the simple differences-in-differences estimate underestimates the size of the effect. Piketty's estimate suggests that in the absence of the reform, the participation rate of mothers with two children (one of whom is under 3) would have been 64.4% in 1997, but because of the measure it stood at just 47.4%.

6.3 Evaluating Policies in a Non-experimental Context: The Role of Selectivity

In practice, the approaches presented are likely to be applicable only in a limited number of cases. Even in cases of certain apparently 'natural' experiments, it has been argued by some authors that differences in the application of reforms across areas or demographic groups may be the result of the treated group having a characteristic that gives rise to the measure being applied, that is being treated is for a reason. This is because polices are implemented for a number of reasons, including targeting help on particular groups such as the poor, the young, single parents, small companies, firms in certain sectors, and so forth. These are all observable features of the beneficiaries. However, participation in a programme may also be on the basis of individuals applying for or signing up for it. Their reasons for doing so may be based on unobserved factors which invalidate the conditional mean independence condition. The non-experimental nature of policy implementation, the absence of a clearly defined control group, and self-selection into programmes are all likely to be features that will need to be taken into account when undertaking policy evaluation in the majority of cases.

However, the ultimate goal is still the same: to estimate the average effect that the policy measure has on an outcome variable. The difficulty encountered in this non-experimental context is how to estimate the average treatment effect in a reliable and robust manner. As already mentioned, the approaches presented above in an experimental context are applicable because they meet two requirements: (a) the treated and control groups can be clearly identified and (b) the conditional mean independence condition $E\left(u_i | \; x_i, d_i\right) = 0$ is satisfied. This last requirement is the key one for unbiased estimation. While there are estimators which provide consistent (that is asymptotically reliable) estimates, no estimator provides unbiased estimates when there is correlation between right-hand side variables and the error term. This section first examines estimation methods when the conditional mean independence condition is violated (sub-section 6.3.1) and then deals with approaches that can be applied when there is no clearly defined control group available in the data (sub-section 6.3.2).

6.3.1 *Selection on 'Unobservables'*

In a large number of evaluations, there is a group that subscribes to and benefits from a programme. There exist non-participants from the same population, and so a control group can be formed, and the difference in mean outcomes for participants and non-participants can be calculated. A useful example here is training programmes, whereby individuals sign up for training (or firms provide training for their workforces) but participation is not 100%. Training should improve the quality of the work done by participants, and this is expected to be reflected in higher earnings *compared to what would have been earned* in the absence of the training. Workers not participating can in principle be used as a control group in order to determine the earnings benefits of training for participants. The problem here is that there has neither been random assignment to the programme nor has the measure been applied on the basis of observable criteria such as age or locality. The conditional mean independence condition will not be satisfied. For example, those workers who stand most to benefit in terms of earnings from training are those that sign up, while those expecting a minor gain do not bother. This is precisely the phenomenon described by the Roy model (see Chapter 4). The difference in earnings between the two groups after the measure is implemented will not be the expected effect of the programme for an individual chosen at random. The true effect will be substantially over-estimated.

In these circumstances, there are two approaches that can be adopted in order to provide consistent (though not unbiased) estimates of training upon earnings. The first is to use a selectivity model. By assuming joint normality of the error terms that determine earnings and participation in the training programme, the properties of the normal distribution can be used to construct a likelihood function for the sample and the effect of training can be estimated using the *control function* approach described in Chapter 4. A second method that can be used, which avoids the need to make restrictive assumptions about the distribution of the error term and the specification of a model to determine programme participation, is instrumental variables. If a variable is correlated with participation but not correlated with the unobserved factors that influence earnings (and which are captured in the error term), then instrumental variables or two stage least squares can be applied.

Consider the simple model adopted above for estimating the average treatment effect:

$$y_i = \alpha + \beta\, d_i + u_i$$

The concern here is the correlation between the dummy variable representing programme participation, d_i, and the error term, u_i. If the dummy instrumental variable z_i is correlated with the participation dummy but not with the error term, then the instrumental variables estimator of β is the Wald estimator, which is obtained when the instrument is a dummy variable though not necessarily the endogenous regressor. In this very simple case, the sample of n observations is divided into two groups: there are n_V individuals for whom $z_i = 1$ and n_N for whom $z_i = 0$. The Wald estimator is given by (see the Appendix for a derivation):

$$\hat{\beta}_{VI} = \frac{\bar{y}^V - \bar{y}^N}{\bar{d}^V - \bar{d}^N}$$

where $\bar{y}^V$and $\bar{y}^N$ are the group means for y_i and defined as $\bar{y}^V = \bar{z}\sum_1^n y_i z_i$ and $\bar{y}^N = (1 - \bar{z})\sum_1^n y_i(1 - z_i)$, respectively, where $\bar{z} = \frac{n_V}{n}$ and $(1 - \bar{z}) = \frac{n_N}{n}$. The instrument weighted means of the participation dummies ($\bar{d}^V$, $\bar{d}^N$) are defined by these same sums with d_i in the place of y_i. These averages are for the variable for each value of the dummy instrumental variable. The denominator simply reflects the degree of correlation between the instrument and the participation dummy. If there is perfect correlation then the denominator equals one.

More generally, for models with several right-hand side variables as well as a treatment dummy, the equivalent two stage least squares procedure can be used. For the model:

$$y_i = \alpha + \beta\, d_i + \theta' x_i + u_i$$

any correlation between d_i and u_i will cause the conditional mean independence condition to fail and lead to biased estimation of the effect of the programme on y_i given by the parameter β. For the same instrument as above, the two stage least squares applies as follows:

(a) Parameters of the following linear regression are estimated by ordinary least squares:

$$d_i = \alpha_0 + \alpha_1\, z_i + \delta' x_i + v_i$$

and the fitted value from this regression is obtained as: $\hat{d}_i = \hat{\alpha}_0 + \hat{\alpha}_1 z_i + \hat{\delta}' x_i$.

(b) In the second stage, this fitted value replaces the programme dummy d_i in the regression for y_i:

$$y_i = \alpha + \beta\, \hat{d}_i + \theta' x_i + u_i^V$$

Note that the parameter of interest in this two stage method is the same (it is still β); it is just estimated by a different method. Furthermore, the standard errors obtained by the application of the OLS to this second stage are not correct (see Chapter 1 above for details).

In the second stage regression, neither of the right-hand side variables, $\hat{d}_i$ and x_i, is correlated with the error term u_i^V created by substituting $\hat{d}_i$ for d_i, and so OLS estimation of β is a consistent (though not unbiased) estimate of the average treatment effect. The error term in the second stage is in fact equal to:

$$u_i^V = \beta\left(d_i - \hat{d}_i\right) + u_i = \beta\, \hat{v}_i + u_i$$

where $\hat{v}_i$ is the OLS residual from the first stage and is necessarily uncorrelated with the regressors included in that stage (z_i and x_i) due to the way in which the OLS estimates are obtained (see Chapter 1); $\hat{d}_i$ is simply a convex combination of an instrumental variable z_i and the exogenous variables x_i, which by definition are uncorrelated (although z_i is only asymptotically uncorrelated) with the original error term u_i. Therefore, in the second stage, asymptotically, the conditional mean independence condition is met because $\lim_{n\to\infty} E\left(u_i^V \mid x_i,\ \hat{d}_i\right) = 0$.

6.3.2 *Selection on 'Observables'*

One of the key requirements when trying to emulate the experimental approach in policy evaluation is the existence of well-defined control group which can be used to create the all-important counter-factual situation—what would have happened to those who are treated if the policy measure had not been implemented. Sometimes it is possible to pick a relatively similar group to that which is treated (for example mothers with one child to compare with mothers with two children). Often eligibility for a programme is determined by institutional rules. An example is where young persons aged 25 or under can receive limited financial aid when out of work, whereas over those over 25 are eligible for a higher amount. Since such aid is likely to affect labour supply, this difference in eligibility can be used to test whether there is jump in the regression line just after the age of 25—and, if so, the size of this jump is an estimate of the difference in financial aid on labour supply. This is called the *regression discontinuity* approach.

However, defining a control group not always possible—especially when the treated group is very heterogeneous. One method of creating a control group is to match each member of the treated group with a person or persons in the non-treated population with the same characteristics. For each match, the difference between the values of y can be calculated and this difference can be aggregated into an average treatment effect. Thus if in a sample of n treated persons, individual i is matched to non-treated individual j, the matching estimator of the average treatment effect is:

$$\Delta_M = \frac{1}{n}\sum_{i=1}^{n}\left(y_i - y_i^j\right)$$

where y_i is the value of the outcome variable for individual i and y_i^j is the value for the individual with whom i is matched.

This approach is valid if there is no correlation between unobserved factors and treatment status—conditional independence—and if there is sufficient overlap in the characteristics between the treated and non-treated populations. The latter is called the *common support* condition. The reliability of this approach will depend on the characteristics or variables used to match individuals and this can be very complicated in calculation terms, since the higher the dimension of the vector on the basis of which individuals are matched, the more difficult it will be to find exact matches. One way of avoiding this dimensionality problem is to aggregate the matching characteristics (x') into a *propensity score*. This is achieved by pooling the treated and non-treated into a single sample estimating the conditional probability of being treated:

$$prob\left(d_i = 1 \mid x_i\right)$$

This can be estimated by a logit or probit model. The estimated probabilities are then used to create matches rather than the vector x. A common method is for each member of the treated group to compare the outcome variable with that for the five nearest observations on the basis of the propensity score, and then aggregate these into an estimate of the average treatment effect. A choice of which weights to use has to be made. Giving everyone involved equal weight would mean following estimator:

$$\Delta_{PM} = \frac{1}{n}\sum_{i=1}^{n}\left(y_i - \frac{1}{5}\sum_{j=1}^{5} y_i^j\right)$$

6.4 Concluding Remarks

The experimental approach to policy evaluation has become very important in labour economics. The extent to which relevant information for policy-makers can be obtained from non-experimental data has been questioned in recent years. However, randomization in labour economics (and other social sciences) is often subject to moral objections and cannot become a widespread basis for empirical investigation. Such an approach often takes the form of a pilot study, but by definition the scope is limited. Natural experiments and quasi-experimental approaches can be useful, but the scope of economic analysis often requires going beyond the kind of information that can be gleaned from an experimental approach, such as indirect and general equilibrium effects or the effects of a measure on well-being.

While emulating the experimental approach was initially seen as a means of examining the effects of policy measures, it has developed into a more general approach for the empirical analysis of labour market behaviour. The emphasis is placed on seeking exogenous variation as a means of identifying causal relations between variables. While from a methodological point of view such an approach is attractive, it tends to produce evidence in the form of case studies. Clearly a large number of different studies of a given relation can represent a body of scientific evidence in favour of one hypothesis or another. However, because it is difficult to generalize from specific cases to the larger picture, some economists have argued that the quasi-experimental approach is of limited interest. On the one hand, it does not address the interesting questions in labour economics, and on the other does not seek to clarify the behavioural mechanisms that give rise to the observed outcomes (see the debate involving Angrist and Pischke (2009), Deaton (2009), Keane (2010), and Imbens (2010)).

Further Reading

The literature on labour market policy evaluation and the related methodological approaches has burgeoned in the last ten years. A key reference is the book by Angrist and Pischke (2009). The statistical bases of alternative approaches to evaluation are very clearly presented by Blundell and Costa Dias (2009). The book by Lee (2004) presents more advanced material on estimation methods and Caliendo (2006) has written a very clear book that covers matching methods. There are useful survey papers in the *Journal of Economic Literature* by Lee and Lemieux (2010) on regression discontinuity and Heckman and Urzua (2010) on methods for programme evaluation. For a critical view of the approach to empirical modelling associated with the quasi-experimental and related methods used in programme evaluation, see Deaton (2009), Keane (2010), and Leamer (2010) along with the reply by Imbens (2010).

Appendix

1. Derivation of the average treatment effect as an OLS estimator

OLS estimation of the parameters of the following model:

$$y_i = \alpha + \beta\, d_i + u_i$$

are given by: $\hat{\alpha} = \bar{y} - \hat{\beta}\bar{d}$ and $\hat{\beta} = \dfrac{\sum_{i=1}^{n}\left(d_i - \bar{d}\right)(y_i - \bar{y})}{\sum_{i=1}^{n}\left(d_i - \bar{d}\right)^2}$.

The sample contains $n = n_0 + n_1$ observations and so $\bar{d} = \frac{n_1}{n}$ is the proportion treated. Using the fact that $\sum_{i=1}^{n}\left(d_i - \bar{d}\right) = 0$, we can write the numerator of $\hat{\beta}$ as

$$\sum_{i=1}^{n}\left(d_i - \bar{d}\right)(y_i - \bar{y}) = \sum_{i=1}^{n}\left(d_i - \bar{d}\right) y_i$$

and expanding, we obtain: $\sum_{i=1}^{n}\left(d_i - \bar{d}\right) y_i = \sum_{i=1}^{n} d_i y_i - \bar{d}\sum_{i=1}^{n} y_i$.

We will use the following property: $\sum_{i=1}^{n} y_i = n\bar{y} = n\left(\frac{n_1}{n}\bar{y}^1 + \frac{n_0}{n}\bar{y}^0\right)$.

Since d_i is a dummy variable for the treated: $\sum_{i=1}^{n} d_i y_i = n_1\bar{y}^1$.

Thus: $\bar{d}\sum_{i=1}^{n} y_i = \frac{n_1}{n}\left(n_1\bar{y}^1 + n_0\bar{y}^0\right)$.

The numerator of the OLS estimator $\hat{\beta}$ is therefore:

$$\begin{aligned}\sum_{i=1}^{n}\left(d_i - \bar{d}\right) y_i &= n_1\bar{y}^1 - \frac{n_1}{n}\left(n_1\bar{y}^1 + n_0\bar{y}^0\right)\\ &= \frac{n_1}{n}\left((n_0 + n_1)\bar{y}^1 - n_1\bar{y}^1 - n_0\bar{y}^0\right)\\ &= \frac{n_1 n_0}{n}\left(\bar{y}^1 - \bar{y}^0\right) \qquad \text{(A.6.1)}\end{aligned}$$

Using similar properties, the denominator can be written:

$$\sum_{i=1}^{n}\left(d_i-\bar{d}\right)^2=\sum_{i=1}^{n}\left(d_i-\bar{d}\right)d_i=\sum_{i=1}^{n}d_i^2-\bar{d}\sum_{i=1}^{n}d_i$$

Since d_i is a dummy variable: $\sum_{i=1}^{n} d_i = n_1$ and $\sum_{i=1}^{n} d_i^2 = n_1$

$$\sum_{i=1}^{n}\left(d_i-\bar{d}\right)^2=n_1-\frac{n_1}{n}n_1=\frac{n_1}{n}\left(n_0+n_1-n_1\right)=\frac{n_1n_0}{n}$$

Thus: $$\hat{\beta}=\frac{\sum_{i=1}^{n}\left(d_i-\bar{d}\right)\left(y_i-\bar{y}\right)}{\sum_{i=1}^{n}\left(d_i-\bar{d}\right)^2}=\frac{\frac{n_1n_0}{n}\left(\bar{y}^1-\bar{y}^0\right)}{\frac{n_1n_0}{n}}=\bar{y}^1-\bar{y}^0$$

2. Derivation of the Wald estimator

The sample of n observations is divided into two groups: there are n_V individuals for whom $z_i = 1$ and n_N for whom $z_i = 0$. The formula for the instrumental variables estimator of β using the dummy variable z_i as an instrument for the dummy d_i in the following linear regression:

$$y_i=\alpha+\beta d_i+u_i$$

is given by:

$$\hat{\beta}_{VI}=\frac{\sum_{i=1}^{n}\left(z_i-\bar{z}\right)\left(y_i-\bar{y}\right)}{\sum_{i=1}^{n}\left(z_i-\bar{z}\right)\left(d_i-\bar{d}\right)}$$

As above, this can be re-written as:

$$\hat{\beta}_{VI}=\frac{\sum_{i=1}^{n}\left(y_i-\bar{y}\right)z_i}{\sum_{i=1}^{n}\left(d_i-\bar{d}\right)z_i}$$

Since z_i is a dummy variable which takes the value 1 for n_V members of the sample, using the result in equation A.6.1, the numerator can be written as:

$$\sum_{i=1}^{n}\left(y_i-\bar{y}\right)z_i=\frac{n_Nn_V}{n}\left(\bar{y}_V-\bar{y}_N\right)$$

Since the denominator is identical in form but with d_i in the place of y_i, it can be expressed as:

$$\sum_{i=1}^{n} \left(d_i - \bar{d}\right) z_i = \frac{n_N n_V}{n} \left(\bar{d}_V - \bar{d}_N\right)$$

The instrumental variables estimator of in this case is then:

$$\hat{\beta}_{VI} = \frac{\bar{y}_V - \bar{y}_N}{\bar{d}_V - \bar{d}_N}$$

This is called the Wald estimator.

Conclusion

The aim of this book has been to present the main econometric techniques used by labour economists. It should serve as a platform for adapting material already encountered in econometrics classes and textbooks to the empirical analysis of labour market phenomena. The passage between the two is not always easy and it is hoped that the material presented in this book will aid this transition. The views expressed here tend to be on whether one technique or another is likely to be more appropriate in the aim of delivering reliable estimates of the parameters of interest. If a choice is made about a particular functional form or distribution, where possible it is advisable to carry out statistical tests of the assumptions made. And it is instructive to compare the results obtained from different approaches (generally starting with the results from a linear regression).

Empirical work, however, is not simply about the use of the relevant econometric technique. Before the practitioner decides on which estimation method to use, (s)he will have thought about which model is appropriate and what data should be used. These matters have not been treated directly here. The origin and characteristics of the data are major components of an empirical study and any serious piece of applied econometrics will begin with an analysis of the properties of the sample which is used. The specification of the model to be estimated is even more important.

There is no conventional wisdom on how to do empirical analysis in labour economics. Several approaches coexist, running from structural models with very tight links to economic theory, to so-called 'model-free' approaches based on emulating the experimental approach. The former approach has the advantage of aiming to model the behavioural mechanisms that underlie observed labour market outcomes. The strong point of the model-free approach is that, unlike the structural approach, causal effects can be identified and estimated without having to make strong and unrealistic assumptions.

In practice, most studies in empirical labour economics lie somewhere in between these two benchmarks and consist of estimating models which are loosely based on theoretical reasoning and specified in a flexible manner so that the data can 'talk'. There has recently been a debate about empirical practice in labour economics, mainly as a result of the emergence and gain in popularity of the experimental type of approach. On the use of the latter, and particularly in relation to the emphasis on using instrumental variables, there is an interesting exchange between Deaton (2010) and Heckman and Urzua (2010) on one side and Imbens (2010) on the other. On the pertinence of the structural approach in the light of recent developments on how applied labour economics should be undertaken (see for example the book by Angrist and Pischke (2009)), there is an interesting contribution by Keane (2010) who argues that the so-called model-free approach is in fact also based on ad hoc assumptions.

These issues are important and concern all labour economists. As with many sub-disciplines of economics, there are a number of standard techniques that are regularly used in labour economics and practitioners need to have these in their toolkit. Knowledge even of certain much-maligned techniques is required in order to know precisely why they are widely criticized. When I was a graduate student, to use a linear probability model instead of a logit or probit model was heresy. These days using a two-stage Heckman approach to sample selection bias is frowned upon. I have even heard, though only recently and not very often, that parametric models can now be dispensed with.

Research into econometric techniques relevant to labour economics is an ongoing activity and from time to time a new technique is added to the toolkit. The existence of more than one means of estimating the parameters of a model implies that it is informative to compare the results obtained from different approaches. In theory we know the circumstances in which an estimator will biased or inconsistent and a judgement can be made if the results diverge. Research in labour economics itself often proceeds through the re-examination of existing studies using alternative methods and data. Exercising a certain degree of suspicion and the critical appraisal of econometric estimates are strongly recommended.

The quotation in the introduction from Leamer of advice to avoid being present when econometric estimates are being *produced*, can be replaced by the following alternative advice: produce a first set of results and assess why they may be unreliable, and *then* try and produce an alternative (more reliable) set of estimates using more appropriate techniques. Subject these estimates to a sensitivity analysis by adding and deleting variables to see how the estimates of parameters of interest change and assess how robust the results actually are. It is worthwhile remembering that research in labour economics often leads to the adoption of policy measures or reforms that have an effect on people's lives.

Bibliography

Allison, Paul (1995), *Survival Analysis Using the SAS System: A Practical Guide*, SAS Institute, North Carolina.

Amemiya, Takeshi (1985), *Advanced Econometrics*, Basil Blackwell, Oxford.

Angrist, Joshua and Alan Krueger (1991), Does compulsory school attendance affect schooling and earnings?, *Quarterly Journal of Economics*, 106, 976–1014.

Angrist, Joshua and Alan Krueger (2001), Instrumental variables and the search for identification: from supply and demand to natural experiments, *Journal of Economic Perspectives*, 15, 69–85.

Angrist, Joshua and Jorn-Steffen Pischke (2009), *Mostly Harmless Econometrics*, Princeton Univeristy Press, Princeton.

Arellano, Manuel (2003), *Panel Data Econometrics*, Oxford University Press, Oxford.

Baltagi, Badi (2008), *Econometric Analysis of Panel Data*, John Wiley, Chichester, Fourth Edition.

Bazen, Stephen and Julie Le Gallo (2009), The state-federal dichotomy in the effects of minimum wages on teenage employment in the United States, *Economics Letters*, 105, 267–9.

Bera, Anil, Carlos Jarque, and Lei-Fung Lee (1984), Testing for normality in limited dependent variable models, *International Economic Review*, 25, 563–78.

Berndt, Ernest (1996), *The Practice of Econometrics: Classical and Contemporary*, Addison Wesley, New York.

Blinder, Alan (1973), Wage discrimination: reduced form and structural estimates, *Journal of Human Resources*, 8, 436–65.

Blundell, Richard and Monica Costa Dias (2009), Alternative approaches to evaluation in empirical microeconomics, *Journal of Human Resources*, 44, 565–640.

Blundell, Richard, Lorraine Dearden, and Barbara Sianesi (2005), Evaluating the effect of education on earnings: models, methods and results from the National Child Development Survey, *Journal of the Royal Statistical Society*, Series A, 168, 473–512.

Buchinsky, Moshe (1998), Recent advances in quantile regression models: a practical guideline for empirical research, *Journal of Human Resources*, 33, 88–126.

Caliendo, Marco (2006), *Microeconometric Evaluation of Labour Market Policies*, Springer Verlag, Berlin.

Cameron, Colin and Pravin Trivedi (2005), *Microeconometrics*, Oxford University Press, Oxford.

Card, David (1999), The causal effect of education on earnings, Chapter 30 in *Handbook of Labor Economics Volume 3*, Elsevier, Amsterdam.

Card, David and Alan Krueger (1994), Minimum wages and employment: a case study of the fast-food industry in New Jersey and Pennsylvania, *American Economic Review*, 84, 772–93.

Card, David and Alan Krueger (1995), *Myth and Measurement: The New Economics of the Minimum Wage*, Princeton University Press, New Jersey.

Cox, David (1972), Regression models and life tables, *Journal of the Royal Statistical Society*, Series B, 34, 187–220.

Davidson, Russell and James MacKinnon (1993), *Estimation and Inference in Econometrics*, Oxford University Press, Oxford.

Davidson, Russell and James MacKinnon (2006), Bootstrap methods in econometrics, in Terence Mills and Kerry Patterson (2006), *Palgrave Handbook of Econometrics*, Palgrave Macmillan, Basingstoke.

Deaton, Angus (1996), *The Analysis of Household Surveys: A Microeconometric Approach to Development Policy*, Johns Hopkins Press, Baltimore.

Deaton, Angus (2009), Instruments, randomisation and learning about development, *Journal of Economic Literature*, 48, 424–55.

Dinardo, John, Nicole Fortin, and Thomas Lemieux (1996), Labor market institutions and the distribution of wages, 1973–92: a semi-parametric approach, *Econometrica*, 64, 1001–44.

Donald, Steven, David Green, and Harry Paarsch (2002), Differences in wage distributions between Canada and the United States: an application of a flexible estimator of distribution functions in the presence of covariates, *Review of Economic Studies*, 67, 609–33.

Fairlie, Douglas (2005), An extension of the Blinder-Oaxaca decomposition technique to logit and probit models, *Journal of Economic and Social Measurement*, 30, 305–16.

Firpo, Sergio, Nicole Fortin, and Thomas Lemieux (2010), Decomposition methods in economics, *Handbook of Labor Economics Volume 4*, Elsevier, Amsterdam, forthcoming.

Goldberger, Arthur (1991), *A Course in Econometrics*, Harvard University Press, Cambridge.

Greene, William (2007), *Econometric Analysis*, Prentice Hall, New York, Sixth Edition.

Hausman, Jerry (1978), Specification tests in econometrics, *Econometrica*, 46, 1251–72.

Hausman, Jerry and Daniel McFadden (1984), A specification test for the multinomial logit model, *Econometrica*, 52, 1219–40.

Hausman, Jerry and David Wise (1977), Social experimentation, truncated distributions and efficient estimation, *Econometrica*, 45, 319–39.

Heckman, James (1979), Sample selection bias as a specification error, *Econometrica*, 47, 153–62.

Heckman, James (1990), Varieties of selection bias, *American Economic Review*, 80, 313–18.

Heckman, James and Sergio Urzua (2010), Comparing IV with structural models: what simple IV can and cannot identify, *Journal of Econometrics*, 156, 27–37.

Heij, Christian, Paul de Boer, Philip Hans Franses, Teun Kloek, and Herman van Dijk (2004), *Econometric Methods with Applications in Busniess and Economics*, Oxford University Press, Oxford.

Imbens, Guido (2010), Better LATE than nothing: some comments on Deaton (2009) and Heckman and Urzua (2009), *Journal of Economic Literature*, 48, 399–423.

Jenkins, Stephen (1995), Easy ways to estimate discrete time duration models, *Oxford Bulletin of Economics and Statistics*, 57, 129–38.

Jenkins, Stephen (2005), Survival Analysis, Unpublished manuscript, Institute for Social and Economic Research, University of Essex.

Juhn, Sun, Kevin Murphy, and David Pierce (1993), Wage inequality and the rise in returns to skill, *Journal of Political Economy*, 101, 410–42.

Kaplan, E. And P. Meier (1958), Nonparametric estimation from incomplete observations, *Journal of the American Statistical Association*, 53, 457–81.

Keane, Michael (2010), Structural vs. atheoretical approaches to econometrics, *Journal of Econometrics*, 156, 3–20.

Kiefer, Nicholas (1988), Econometric duration data and hazard function, *Journal of Economic Literature*, 26, 646–79.

Koenker, Roger (2005), *Quantile Regression*, Econometric Society Monograph, Cambridge University Press, Cambridge.

Koenker, Roger and Kim Bassett (1978), Regression quantiles, *Econometrica*, 46, 33–50.

Lalonde, Robert (1986), Evaluating the econometric evaluations of training programmes with experimental data, *American Economic Review*, 76, 604–20.

Lancaster, Tony (1992), *The Econometric Analysis of Duration Data*, Cambridge University Press, Cambridge.

Leamer, Edward (1978), *Specification Searches: Ad hoc Inference with Non-experimental Data*, Wiley, New York.

Leamer, Edward (1983), Let's take the "con" out of econometrics, *American Economic Review*, 73, 31–43.

Leamer, Edward (2010), Tantalus on the road to asymptotia, *Journal of Economic Perspectives*, 24, 31–46.

Lee, Myoung-Hae (2005), *Microeconometrics for Policy, Program and Treatment Effects*, Oxford University, Oxford.

Lee, David and Thomas Lemieux (2010), Regression discontinuity designs in economics, *Journal of Economic Literature*, 48, 281–355.

Lemieux, Thomas (2002), Decomposing changes in wage distributions: a unified approach, *Canadian Journal of Economics*, 35, 646–88.

Lemieux, Thomas (2006), The "Mincer equation" thirty years after *Schooling, Experience and Earnings*, Chapter 11 in Shoshana Grossbard (2006), *Jacob Mincer: A Pioneer of Modern Labor Economics*, Springer Verlag, Berlin.

Machado, José and José Mata, (2005), Counterfactual decompositions of changes in wage distributions using quantile regression, *Journal of Applied Econometrics*, 20, 445–65.

Maddala, G.S. (1983), *Limited Dependent and Qualitative Variables in Econometrics*, Cambridge University Press, Cambridge.

Matyas, Laszlo and Patrick Sevestre (2008), *The Econometrics of Panel Data*, Springer Verlag, Berlin. Third Edition.

Melino, Angelo (1982), Testing for sample selection bias, *Review of Economic Studies*, 49, 151–3.

Meyer, Bruce (1990), Unemployment insurance and unemployment spells, *Econometrica*, 58, 757–82.

Mincer, Jacob (1974), *Schooling, Experience and Earnings*, National Bureau of Economic Research, Columbia University Press, New York.

Moulton, Brent (1998), An illustration of a pitfall encountered in estimating the effects of aggregate variables on micro units, *Review of Economics and Statistics*, 72, 334–8.

Neuman, Shoshana and Ronald Oaxaca (2004), Wage decompositions with selectivity-corrected wage equations: a methodological note, *Journal of Economic Inequality*, 2, 3–10.

Neumark, David and William Wascher (2006), Minimum wages and employment, *IZA Discussion Paper* No. 2570, Bonn, Germany.

Nickell, Stephen (1979), Estimating the probability of leaving unemployment, *Econometrica*, 47, 1249–66.

Oaxaca, Ronald (1973), Male-female differentials in urban labor markets, *International Economic Review*, 14, 673–709.

Oaxaca, Ronald, and Michael Ransom (1994), On discrimination and the decomposition of wage differentials, *Journal of Econometrics*, 61, 5–21.

Piketty, Thomas (1998), L'impact des incitations financières au travail sur les comportements individuels: une estimation pour le cas français, *Economie et Prevision*, 132, 1–35.

Pudney, Stephen (1989), *Modelling Individual Choice*, Basil Blackwell, Oxford.

Ramsey, James (1969), Tests of specification error in classical linear least squares regression, *Journal of the Royal Statistical Society*, Series B, 31, 350–71.

Salant, William (1977), Search theory and duration data: a theory of sorts, *Quarterly Journal of Economics*, 91, 39–57.

Sargan, James (1964), Wages and prices in the UK: a study in econometric methodology, reprinted as Chapter 10 in David Hendry and Kenneth Wallis (1984), *Econometrics and Quantitative Economics*, Blackwell, Oxford.

Stock, James, Jonathan Wright, and Motohiro Yogo (2002), A survey of weak instruments and weak identification in generalised method of moments, *Journal of Business and Economics Statistics*, 20, 518–29.

Stock, James and Motohiro Yogo (2002), Testing for weak instruments in linear IV regression, National Bureau of Economic Research, Technical Working Paper No. 284.

Taubman, Paul (1976), Earnings, education, genetics and environment, *Journal of Human Resources*, 11, 447–61.

Tobin, James (1958), Estimation of relationships for limited dependent variables, *Econometrica*, 26, 24–36.

Vella, Francis (1998), Estimating models with sample selection bias: a survey, *Journal of Human Resources*, 33, 127–69.

White, Halbert (1980), A heteroscedasticity-consistent covariance matrix estimator and a direct test for heteroscedastcity, *Econometrica*, 48, 817–38.

Wooldridge, Jeffrey (2002), *Econometrics with Cross Section and Panel Data*, MIT Press, Cambridge, United States.

Index